My Hi-De-High Life

Before, After and During Su Pollard

Peter Keogh

First published in 2014 by Apex Publishing Ltd
12A St. John's Road, Clacton on Sea
Essex, CO15 4BP, United Kingdom
www.apexpublishing.co.uk

Please email any queries to Chris Cowlin:
mail@apexpublishing.co.uk

Print layout by
Andrews UK Limited
www.andrewsuk.com

Copyright © 2014 Peter Keogh

The author has asserted his moral rights

All rights reserved. This book is sold subject to the condition, that no part of this book is to be reproduced, in any shape or form. Or by way of trade, stored in a retrieval system or transmitted in any form or by any means, electronic, mechanical, photocopying, recording, be lent, re-sold, hired out or otherwise circulated in any form of binding or cover other than that in which it is published and without a similar condition, including this condition being imposed on the subsequent purchaser, without prior permission of the copyright holder.

Contents

Bush Baby	1
School Daze	7
Sexual Curiosity - and Abuse	14
Following Father's Footsteps	18
'Arrested' Development - Africa	21
Gay - Coming Out	29
Showbiz - Stars and Others	35
Chasing 'Tammy' - LA 'Misadventures'	48
Perth - Playhouse 'Stars' - London	53
Claridges - Charges - Court	59
Hi-de-Hi! and Me	65
Wedding Bell Blues - Trial by Jury	71
Mr. & Mrs. Keogh and the Press	79
Married Life - Princess Diana and 'Others'	93
West End - 'Me and My Girl'	99
Top of the Pops - 'Starting Together'	106
Broadway - almost a 'Funny Girl'	109
This is 'Our' Life	114
Sacha, Separation, Death and Divorce	118
Life after Su - Health Scares	125
'Unsinkable' Debbie Reynolds and Me	132
Cancer and other 'hiccups'	142
Hey, Mr. Producer - again	145
Commitment - Heart Attacks - Bye-de-Bye	150

For my Mother, Nita, with my eternal thanks for her love, support and never-ending patience for her black sheep son. Finally, I think I have made her just a little proud!

Special thanks to Jenny Powers and Debbie Reynolds

Forewords

Peter Keogh's book is sensational reading. He has led a remarkable life and has made many lasting friendships. Peter is loved by so many, including me.
Debbie Reynolds

Peter's book is a fun and insightful read. If I had one reservation it's that I'm not in it enough, but living with him for seven years was a roller coaster of a ride. To know Peter is to love him.
John Frost

What a great and empowering read. I was racing to the next adventure with a fixed smile of joy and delight in this spirited, brave and loving memoir. This is Peter's 'yellow brick road' - a lion with courage from the beginning.
Tina Bursill

Preface

I have been notorious all of my life for adhering to the premise of 'on the mind, on the tongue'. I don't seem to have any warning light, which caused me a great deal of anguish and trouble when I was younger, but as I 'matured', and I use the word loosely, it became less of an issue, and I sense it probably has now become an endearing quality, of sorts. As I grew into my more sensible years, I discovered I had the ability to fairly accurately recall details of my life; some painful, some full of joy.

Growing up gay in Australia in the 1950s was traumatic. Along with the conflicting emotion of discovering who I was, there were episodes of physical and sexual abuse, which shaped my adult life. Moving to Sydney on my own in the 1960s and '70s was the chance to explore my sexuality. It was a time of self-discovery during which I really tried to be true to myself but mostly without success. There were many incidents that sent me reeling, including being arrested by 'pretty police' in the Prince Edward Theatre, but I also made deep friendships and had such enormous fun.

Once in Sydney, with bravado, I mustered the courage to be completely open about my homosexuality and 'came out'. That decision had its consequences, but working full time in show business, being gay was never a problem. I met, worked with, and loved, some of the biggest names in Australian show business. I also met visiting overseas artists - some household names - who eventually led me to London where I had further 'adventures', including being charged with theft and facing a trial by jury that garnered as much press coverage that year as the Falklands War.

I also married one of the biggest British female stars of the decade. Why? Well you will need to read further! But that marriage led to some intense life-changing outcomes and my rushing headlong into experiences with people I had only ever dreamed about meeting, including royalty. My life has been a long, twisting roller coaster journey crammed with some amazing life experiences; good, bad and embarrassing. I have had adventures with some of the best people on earth - some of them huge Hollywood stars, others my dearest friends and family. There have been highs and lows, hits and flops, but it's never been dull. I remember reading somewhere once that you have to go back to your beginning to understand the ending. So here as I hurtle towards 'the ending' is what I remember about that roller coaster journey.

I hope that you enjoy the ride!

My Hi-De-High Life

Bush Baby

This tale starts a long time ago in a small town called Mount Barker, about 200 miles south of Perth, the capital city of Western Australia. Then it was mainly a farming town but today boasts some of the best wineries in the state. There was one main street with one pub and lots of pine trees - whenever I smell a pine tree today I am immediately transported back to Mount Barker. Dad; Douglas Edward Keogh, was from a prosperous and industrious family. His father owned a grocery, the main store in town, where you could buy almost anything. Dad, who was the second eldest of eight children in a very, very, very strong Roman Catholic family, worked in the shop with some of his brothers and sisters. Their faith was the backbone of their lives. He was definitely a man's man - he played in the local football team and was extremely handsome, fit and highly respected. He could also put his hand to anything. He served in the army with distinction from 1939 to 1943 in the 2nd 16th Battalion and fought all over Europe until he was shot in the foot in New Guinea and repatriated back to Perth. I remember him being very proud of his time in the army and of the friends he made - and lost - but he found it very difficult to talk at length about any of the horrors he experienced.

At the same time Mum; Nita Jean Tonkin, the eldest of four children, was working as a telephonist at the Mount Barker Post Office. Her father was the station master, the senior official in charge of a railway station. She was very pretty and rather shy but also excellent at almost anything she tried. Religion was NOT the backbone of the Tonkin family, although they were a strong if not openly affectionate family. They were anti-Catholic and almost had conniptions when Mum and Dad started to 'court'. However, in spite of these family objections their love grew and they ended up marrying in the Perth suburb of Cottesloe in May, 1943. Mum wore a beautiful dress - this I know because she kept it for years and I remember trying it on several times when I was very young. I was fascinated by all the fabric-covered buttons and I loved to twirl around the room in it.

The newlyweds started their new lives in the beachside suburb of Scarborough where, in a little over a year, on 15 August, 1944, I was born, causing great distress to Mum for two reasons. Firstly, because she went into labour while Dad was at work and had to catch a taxi by herself to the hospital which was about half an hour from their home - over a gravel road. The anxious taxi driver took to the gravel so fast that Mum was violently thrown around. Then it was my turn! Weighing in at ten pounds, her obstetrician said I was so big I should be given a steak because my hands were big enough to hold a knife and fork. I was not a particularly happy baby and apparently whenever poor Dad attempted to hold me I would either try to scratch him or stick my fingers in his eyes - it must have been very difficult for him.

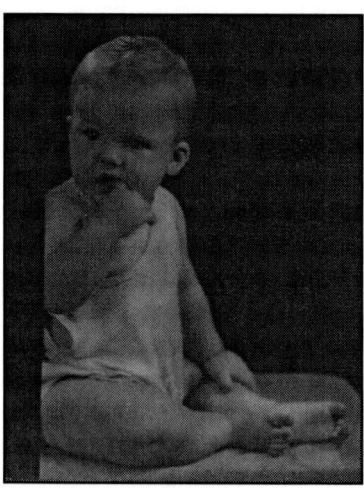

At about 18 months.

Not long after I was born, they moved back to Mount Barker and finally to Kendenup, a one horse - occasionally two horse, town about 20 miles north of Mount Barker. Mum and Dad had a small asbestos home on a hill above my grandparents' rather posh home, which was about half a mile away.

Dad worked hard on their small farm. I was busy trying to avoid all the farm chores preferring instead to lie on the floor reading newspapers and listening to Miss Margaret Graham's Children's Hour on the 'wireless'. One year Mum and Dad organised to have her wish me a Happy Birthday on the show - I was the happiest kid in the world. It was an early brush with 'showbiz'. What I remember most about living on the farm were the heat, dust, snakes and goannas; the magpies swooping and pulling out bits of my hair making my head bleed as I walked past their nests and the horrible 'dunny' - outside toilet - which the 'ice cream man' used to come and empty weekly into his big tank truck. I have no idea why he was called the 'ice cream man'!

The following photo was taken when Mum was very pregnant with me and I love it because it shows a side of Dad that one rarely saw, probably after I came into his life, but they both look so happy and in love. I told Mum that they look like Ma and Pa Kettle!

In 1947, my sister Jetnnifer was born. I can't recall any special feelings of affection or jealousy - she was just not there one day and there the next. The first time I felt some kind of feelings, they turned out to be scary. When she was about two-years-old, I found her under the kitchen table covered in blood. She used to suck her thumb badly and her sharp thumb nail had torn open the roof of her mouth. Mum and Dad rushed her to hospital where they put splints on her hands so she couldn't put them into her mouth. They put her in an enclosed cot that looked very much like a fly-wire cell. It broke my heart when we had to say goodbye to her and leave her in the hospital - we could hear her desperate cries all the way to the car park.

At age four I was sent to St. Joseph's Convent in Mount Barker, about half an hour's drive from home. Dad made a bus shelter for me from an empty crate that our fridge had arrived in and every morning I used to walk down the hill to the highway and wait there, on my own, for the school bus. It didn't worry me at all - it was simply what I had to do to get to school. One of my funniest school stories was when I was just five-years-old and perhaps it hinted at things to come. Mum received a

call from the nuns asking her to send Dad to pick me up because under my uniform I had worn one of my aunt's brassieres, which had fallen off my shoulders and down to my shorts with a size D-cup falling out of each leg. Apparently they told Dad that I needed treatment because I might be turning into a homosexual. Never! I remember poor Dad picking me up from school and driving me home and not a word being said, which was probably a good thing but how he must have felt I can't begin to imagine.

I had my first real brush with 'showbiz' at St Joseph's. The school concert was held at the Mt Barker Town Hall and I was to be a French sailor. Mum, who was a dab hand at making our clothes, had made me a silk costume with a blue beret complete with a red pom-pom. But there was not enough elastic in the pants and down they fell mid-event - and me with them. All I can remember is trying to pull them up and the material being very shiny and slippery and the whole hall laughing loudly, which I think I liked. I certainly adored everything else about the event - the beautiful house curtain, the coloured spotlights, the smell of the make-up, the excitement building as the curtain was about to go up and I felt terminally sad when it was all over. I can't recall if Dad was in the audience that night - I hope not!

Living in the 'bush' did nothing for me as a child - it just left me cold. Dad and Mum did all the right things to try and make me happy but usually to no avail. I was, however, the best dressed kid in the 'bush' thanks to Mum's various skills. I also had the most unruly hair - two crowns - so every morning before I left the house to go to school Mum would plaster my hair down with paraffin oil, which attracted hordes of blowflies. You could always tell when I was coming down the road because I was wearing a halo of flies buzzing around my head.

There was one particularly upsetting event that I still have nightmares about. Dad and I were visiting my Uncle Eric's and Aunty Launa's large farm and they both decided that it would be a growing experience for me to watch them slaughter a couple of sheep, which they did for their own food a couple of times a year. Under duress, I watched as they cut the throat of the first sheep. I immediately started to scream uncontrollably as I ran to the orchard and collapsed under a tree, inconsolable for hours.

On a lighter note my sister, Jenny, and I were playing in my uncle's barn where he kept a lot of chooks - chickens. We were both curious about how eggs happened so we lay down under some hens that were nesting on a sort of raised section and after a while actually ended up seeing an egg being laid. It was intriguing to us watching how the shell sort of gathered in the chook's bottom or whatever, and then a perfectly formed warm egg dropped out. We were so excited we ran with the egg to show mum and Dad and they were banned from cooking it - might be a chicken inside. It was a much more pleasant experience than the sheep episode!

When I turned six we all moved back to the 'big smoke' of Perth and lived in a home I loved in East Fremantle, a middle-class suburb not far from the port city of Fremantle. I adored the house, which had a huge mulberry tree in the back yard. Mum tells me that I wouldn't eat them because I told her they had 'hairs growing out of them'. A very picky child! We also had a huge garage/shed that to me was my own personal theatre - I just loved it - and I spent hours there imagining I was putting on a show. I was inspired by the movie *Babes in Arms* in which Mickey and Judy did just that. If they could do it, so could I! Mum had numerous bouts of ill health, so my aunty Barbara would come to look after my sister and me. I vividly remember being a bit cheeky - I believe I called her a 'bloody bitch' - so she proceeded to drag me into the laundry and fill my mouth with soap and water until I was literally frothing and blowing bubbles. I never forgot that day nor was I cheeky again, to her at least. At that time there were trams running down the middle of Canning Highway and I used to catch one every day to school at Our Lady of Fatima, for a penny. It was about two miles from our home. I loved it there; the nuns were kind and I loved the smell of the place... must have been the chalk or something. Nothing special happened at school but across the road from our home was a cinema and Mum and Dad liked to take us to the movies every Saturday night. Sometimes the best part of the night would be when the movie finished and I would pretend to be asleep because then I was gently carried home by Mum or Dad and tucked into bed, which I loved. It made me feel so safe. There were two movies that stand out in my memory. The first was *Annie Get Your Gun* - when I arrived home I professed to Mum and Dad that when I grow up I was going to marry Howard Keel AND Betty Hutton. Then we saw *Two Weeks with Love* and I was smitten with a funny little lass running all over screen singing 'Aba Daba Honeymoon' and 'Row, Row, Row', she made me laugh. Her name was Debbie Reynolds!

School Daze

We moved around quite a bit over the years because Dad had a couple of positions that necessitated a transfer - it usually meant that he was climbing up the corporate ladder. Next stop was Mosman Bay, a very exclusive suburb on the Swan River where Dad built his own home - quite a feat for its time and rather grand. I used to play around the house as it was being built and as the builders carried tiles up ladders I used to play underneath and was fascinated by the view up the builders' shorts - I found it 'intriguing' - and I was eight! I spent two years at Iona Convent with my sister where the nuns made me their pet. I was a cute freckled blonde, very shy and with a developing stammer so they were very protective. At Iona I had a crush on one of the female boarders the same age as me and sent a perfectly innocent little love note that one of the nuns intercepted and, once again, Dad was called and that was nipped in the bud. Bit sad really. I was also an altar boy at the parish church and loved learning the Latin responses to the priest; the smell of the incense; the candles - the theatricality of it all. But I especially loved what I had to wear; a cassock and surplice, similar to a choir boy's outfit. How I swished around the sacristy before and after Mass. It felt just like being on stage with the congregation as my audience.

Sadly, three of those nuns from Iona and one of the parish priests drowned a few years later when their little boat turned over not far from where I now live in Mandurah. Five nuns and the priest ventured out into the bay in a small fiberglass dinghy with an outboard motor. At about 4.00 pm a strong wind capsized the boat tipping them all into the water in their habits, which were very cumbersome in those days. As the boat upturned, one of the nuns, aged 50, almost immediately had a heart attack and drowned. A little while later another nun, aged only 38, slipped away and drowned while the third nun, aged 26, managed to cling on until about midnight when, sadly, she too lost her grip and drowned. The priest was able to give them the last rites before they died and his body was found, with the two survivors, tangled up in the rope attached to the outboard motor. It was a terrible tragedy which affected us all. By coincidence, there is in fact a lovely memorial to them at the Mandurah Performing Arts Centre.

Mum was in and out of hospital during this time and I used to stay with my Aunt, Uncle and cousins in Napier Street, Cottesloe, an ocean beach suburb. They called me Piccolo Pete and I loved them all so much, I often didn't want to go back to my own home. On 5 November every year they had a Guy Fawkes Night and the whole of Napier Street was closed to traffic - a huge bonfire was built and the street came together with food, drink and fireworks. There was a great feeling of being a part of the community, which I find lacking today. Whenever Mum had to go to hospital I worried beyond words that she would die, so every night I would get on my knees and pray to God to please let me die before Mummy or Daddy because I felt as though I couldn't live without them.

At nine I was enrolled at the strict St. Louis Jesuit College in Claremont where the motto was 'Give me a boy until he is seven and I will give you a man'. These days, considering the number of child abuse cases that have come to light, this could have several interpretations, but thankfully nothing of that kind happened to me at St. Louis. I actually did very well in spite of being terminally shy and with my daily worsening stammer, though I did attract the attention of bullies. The kid I sat next to - I have never forgotten his name - tortured me with the pointy end of his compass, every day scratching a bit more of his initial into my upper leg, under my shorts so no one ever saw it. It still puzzles me as to why I didn't speak up. All I can remember feeling was immense pain and fear. We didn't have tissues in those days so I had to use my handkerchief to blot the blood and then throw it away. Finally, to ensure his initials would stay, he put ink on the cuts and soon my thigh grew to an enormous size, badly infected. After telling Dad what happened he took me to the Prefect of Studies, Fr. Williams, but the outcome of that meeting was that he inferred I had done it to myself. I was hurt beyond words. After that I used to spend every lunch hour hiding under the huge trees in the school yard. They are still there and whenever I drive past the school, which is a retirement village now, it is as if it all happened yesterday. I was alone at school except occasionally meeting up with my cousin, who was the same age but outgoing and sporty with lots of friends. As I got older my stammer worsened and often when I was asked a question I would attempt to answer as my body convulsed trying to get the words out. Finally, I would wet my pants out of fear and embarrassment and then be made to stand in front of the whole class with a large pee stain growing through my khaki shorts. At the end of the year the school put on a concert which was usually a Gilbert & Sullivan piece where the boys would play both male and female roles - one of them was me! I remember being backstage in costume one night as one of the 'maidens' - and looking rather fetching if I do say so myself - when Fr. Williams, who disliked me intensely, looked me up and down and with a nasty sneer said, "You look exactly like a girl," then rolled his eyes and walked away. I think I was sort of pleased but also very hurt by his tone. However, I did have a couple of heroes in Mr. Bartels and Mr. - now Father - Noel Bradford, who reached out to me in various ways to make me feel worthwhile. But even with their support, I was indescribably shy and had a bit of an overbite to add to my woes.

I used to ride to school on a bicycle, a journey of several miles, and I loved it. I used to sing all the way there and back as I coasted down the steep hills of Mosman Bay. Sadly on the way home one day I fell off my bike and my arm went through the spokes of the front wheel. My arm was clearly broken - it was bent like a 'V'. A passing motorist stopped and drove me home and then Mum and Granddad took me straight to Bethesda Hospital to have it operated on. As I was being checked in I decided it was not for me so I did a runner, out of the hospital and down the street like a jet. However, Granddad was even faster. He caught me and dragged me back kicking and screaming. It was actually a ghastly experience. In those days they used chloroform, which they slowly dropped onto a cloth mask held tightly over the face. It had the most disgusting smell and its effect was revolting.

Dad and Mum were very concerned about my increasingly bad stammer and my lack of friends, plus they felt my sexuality was going to become a problem as I started to reach puberty. They sent me to a child psychologist and speech therapist. The psychologist showed me the Rorschach ink blots and all I could see were profiles of Hollywood stars - truly! The speech therapist made me hold a tissue, I think it was, against the wall and I had to talk forcefully enough to stop the tissue from falling. Didn't help one tiny bit - poor Mum and Dad! They must have despaired when they received the psychologist's reports. I don't think I ever had any expression of any sort on my face; it was just barricaded against the world.

During my last year at St Louis I would often wag school and go to the movies in Perth. At that time the sessions were continuous so I would see the same movie a couple of times. I was slowly becoming sexually curious and would very occasionally have a quick fondling experience with a fellow student. All innocent really but a growing curiosity and none of it towards girls. Looking back at my school years in Perth I never had a friend. I was never invited to anyone's house or party and never had one of my own - I guess it was because I had no one to invite. However, I really enjoyed my own company and would spend quite happy hours swapping comics, cutting out movie stars' photos, pretending I was a priest and saying mass in the laundry, or riding my push bike for hours. My other escape was writing little plays then setting up the back verandah as a stage, using dad's slide projector as a follow spot. Then I would have my sister play all the roles - poor cow! I remember being rather taken by *Tarzan* movies at that time - can't imagine why. I made a loincloth from two of Mum's tiny bath flannels joined with safety pins at the hip and proceeded to swing from the clothes line doing Tarzan yells. One of our female neighbours complained bitterly to Mum that I was being indecent, dressed in just those flannels I suggested to Mum that the neighbour had no right to even have been watching.

In 1953, for the Queen's Coronation, Mum, Dad my sister and I sat up very late at night to listen to the whole ceremony on the 'Little Nipper' wireless and I have to say the pictures we had to create in our minds very closely matched the films we later saw, so expert were the announcers at describing the scene. Then in 1954 the Queen came to Perth and the whole school lined up on the highway to watch her pass by - at such speed it could have been anyone in the car - by the time we had raised our flags to wave she was gone. However, the whole state was gripped with excitement and we actually got a bit teary as we all went to the ocean to watch her leave Australia on the 'Gothic'. The whole family stood there until the ship disappeared into the horizon. She certainly left her mark on me. I adored the way she made speeches so I used to write my own and once again, in our backyard, I would stand on a chair wearing a pair of Mum's long gloves and start the speech with 'My husband and I...', a preview of things to come I guess when I was actually invited to Buckingham Palace many years later.

About this time I had my first brush with death and loss. I had a dog called Sandy and I adored every hair of him. He loved me too and whenever I couldn't cope at home or at school. I'd tell Sandy my troubles and he understood when no one else did. One day I was in my bedroom when I heard a screech of brakes and Mum's scream. I ran outside to see my little Sandy jump up from under a car howling like a baby, run to Mum's feet, lie down and die. Dad grabbed me and took me inside the house while they picked up his tiny body and rushed him to the Cottesloe Veterinary Clinic just in case. When they came home without him, I ran from room to room sobbing my heart out, holding his lead and one of his toys. We only had two photos of him which I still have.

What destroyed me as much as his dying was the fact that at school we were taught that only humans have souls and when an animal dies it just disappears into nowhere - forever! I couldn't bear the thought of my little pal's spirit disappearing like that when it was very much alive in my heart. I even asked my parish priest whether he thought that if a dog was special, like my Sandy, God might allow it into heaven. At night I would sleep with Sandy's rug because it still had some of his hair on it and his lovely smell. I cried so much, Mum and Dad became quite worried. Ever since then loss is the hardest thing in the world for me to cope with.

In 1957, Dad was transferred to Sydney and I attended the Jesuit St Aloysius College in Milson's Point, almost under the Sydney Harbour Bridge. I adored this school and I started coming out of my shell a bit. I started getting very good grades. I was fairly popular and I discovered how being funny made me feel liked and would also help me get out of the scrapes I got myself into - still does! I met a student from my class at St Aloysius a couple of years ago and he said that all he can remember of me was me doing impressions of the teachers behind the lid of my desk. I also had a fling-ette with a fellow pupil; furtive fondles in a theatrette at the Easter Show was about all we did, but it made me feel liked. I was even in the school cadets and got a prize for being the fastest to strip and put back together some type of gun. I can't remember which type, although it might have been a Bren - a big thing!

I was even quite adept in the sports arena at St Aloysius, mainly athletics but also was playing rugby where my position was second row in the scrum, in other words I was bent over hugging a person each side and had my nose practically up some other kid's bottom! I used to just close my eyes and push until the melee had finished and hope that no part of me would end up damaged. During cricket matches, which I found deadly boring, I would be fielding which meant standing way out on the field watching and waiting for any cricket ball to head my way. However, I was so bored that I used to be singing and dancing as I waited for the ball to come my way and when it did it always flew right past a dancing me. I lost count of the number of times that I would hear - 'Keogh, the bloody ball's gone right passed you - AGAIN!'

Every weekend my sister and I would go to see a movie somewhere, usually a musical; we were real pals at that time. Sadly, over the years, the dynamics of our family changed and we are now no longer speaking - probably both too stubborn to change. She has a large family that keeps growing with grandchildren, whom I will never meet. So she will be surrounded by a caring family as she gets older but we will just have to agree to disagree and get on with our lives. I have no time or inclination now to allow any unnecessary negativity in my life.

My sister, Jenny, Dad and me in St. Aloysius uniform in Hyde Park Sydney after Mass at St. Mary's Cathedral hence the black knees.

Sexual Curiosity - and Abuse

Then Dad was transferred to Melbourne and I attended Xavier College, yet another Jesuit establishment and not a particularly happy time for lots of reasons. Burgeoning sexuality, no confidence, and being 'interfered with' by a teacher. I was struggling with mathematics, so I would stay back after school for extra help. However, this much older teacher would sit beside me and as I was working, he would slowly undo my fly buttons with his ruler. He had a field day with his hand while I was like a statue, unable to move, barely able to breathe. After a few weeks of this and me having screaming nightmares - I used to scream so much my voice would disappear and staying in a park near school all day, too scared to face him, he disappeared... no clues as to where or why!

The next incident of a similar nature involved the performer Tommy Steele, of whom I had been a huge fan for ages. He was in Melbourne appearing at the Tivoli Theatre and I plucked up the courage to go to the stage door to ask if I could get his autograph, in my school uniform and aged 14, I hasten to add. One of his entourage - his name is also engraved in my mind - invited me in to Tommy's dressing room where we had a chat and I met Tommy. Then they both asked me if I wanted to come back to their apartment near the theatre and I could have a signed copy of his 'Tommy the Toreador' recording. Of course I was thrilled and agreed. Tommy was charming and gave me the recording and left saying that the other person would ensure that I got to the train station safely because he didn't want me roaming town on my own. As soon as Tommy left I was told to wait while this chap got his coat. After about five minutes he came back into the room stark naked and sat beside me with an album of cuttings of Tommy's reviews and opened it so that half was on my lap and the other half on his and proceeded to give me a complete lesson in oral sex. I felt as though my whole body not just my mouth had been ravaged. I felt so unclean and had terrible fears about all kinds of diseases. However, once again I froze but did what I was told until he had finished with me and then was taken to the station. It was a total mystery why these things happened to me, I even started to wonder if I was subconsciously inviting it all somehow. I was totally confused and started to feel very guilty, plus scared because I knew it was a mortal sin - which meant eternal fire in hell!

However, in spite of all the guilt of those experiences, they also aroused my curiosity in gay sex. About a year later, on the way home from school, I changed trains at Flinders Street Station in Melbourne where I was followed by an older chap - by older I mean about 25 - I was only 15. He chatted and wasn't threatening at all; in fact he was handsome and charming. He said he lived just about half a mile away and asked if I would I like to go back to his place. In spite of being very scared, my curiosity got the better of me and I agreed. My heart was pounding; I was even a little excited. I can vaguely remember getting undressed and getting into bed and fumbling around for an hour or so - no penetration of any sort and I didn't actually find it an unpleasant experience. When I arrived home quite late I just got undressed in the dark and threw my underwear and socks into the laundry basket. Next morning Mum came to me with a big pair of strange looking underpants in her hands asking me were they came from - I had left the chap's flat in a hurry and in the dark and ended putting on his underpants not mine. I think I told Mum that I got changed after sports - which I NEVER went to - and must have put them on by mistake. Poor Mum! I know she was quite stressed about the incident but to her credit nothing further was ever said.

I have always had, and still do have, issues with physical closeness and have never been one who likes to hug or to be hugged, which I know has upset some, probably all, of my partners. I had absolutely no confidence of any sort. If I did go to bed with somebody I was often surprised that they were still there in the morning and was terrified to either break wind or have bad breath, so I would pretend to be asleep until they were sound asleep and then I would sneak out of bed, go to the toilet, clean my teeth, do my hair and lacquer it so every hair was perfectly in place and then creep back into bed and pretend to be asleep. One morning, the person I was in bed with woke up, rolled over, looked at me and said, "Christ, how do you do it? You look better now than when you went to bed!"

However, there were also some wonderful fun times. In Melbourne there was, and still is, a terrible old barn called Festival Hall, which was used for boxing and also for visiting artists from overseas. I remember when Connie Francis came to town her movie *Where the Boys Are* was playing in the city so my sister and I went to the afternoon session of the movie and then rushed across town to see her 'live' at Festival Hall. I don't think she was used to performing to such large crowds because whenever they screamed, as one did at those concerts, she kept telling us all to please hush up because she couldn't sing with all the noise. We also saw at the top of their career Bobby Darin, Frankie Avalon, Brenda Lee, Chubby Checker and Hugh O'Brian as 'Wyatt Earp' at the Princess Theatre. He did the whole show as the 'Wyatt Earp' character - him and his horse, a few songs and a mock bar room brawl. It was not particularly entertaining but he was very handsome, as was his horse, which I actually think was more talented than Hugh! One performer though who really knocked my socks off, which surprised me because I wasn't a huge fan, was Jack Benny. The support act was the wonderful Australian entertainer Lorrae Desmond. After the interval and with no announcement Jack sauntered onto the stage and just stood there, arms folded, staring at the audience for ages. He had every single member of the audience, especially me, eating out of the palm of his hand. Totally and utterly a STAR!

I was also a huge *Mickey Mouse Club* fan and fully-eared 'Mouseketeer' fan. The show was as big in Australia as it was in America and I was glued to the television nightly to watch the show. I especially adored Annette Funicello. When they announced that the Mouseketeers were coming to Melbourne

I was beside myself, only saddened that Annette wasn't among them. I actually even had my own Mouseketeer top, which was my footy shirt on which I sewed 'PETE'. When the six of them arrived, all in their 20s but in full Mickey Mouse Club uniform, ears included, they were mobbed at the airport and when they were driven through the CBD, on the back of a big float, record crowds blocked the streets.

I honestly don't know how I managed it but I found out where they were staying and just walked into the hotel while they were in the foyer and struck up a conversation with Mouseketeer Cheryl Holdridge. She introduced me to the other Mouseketeers and I spent most of that night chatting with them; Bobby Burgess, Tommy Cole, Doreen Tracey, 'little' Karen Pendleton and Cubby O'Brien - we all just seemed to click. Cheryl even gave me her home address to visit if I was in Sherman Oaks, California, which at that time seemed a totally impossible dream for a shy 16- year-old. Little did I know that it would be overseas where my life would take its incredible turns!

Following Father's Footsteps

Dad and I were not as close as I think in his heart of hearts he would have liked and believe me; I truly tried in so many ways to be the man he wanted me to be. Suppressing all of the deep feelings I was having about a life that Dad understood nothing about was as hard as it could possibly be. Mum was in the middle and I think she knew that I was not going to follow the same path as Dad, that in fact it would be a path that would hurt Dad enormously. She wouldn't - couldn't - take sides so it must have been horrible for her. I think it was around this time that they decided to have another child, and it was the best thing they could have done but it didn't solve any of my growing issues.

At about the same time of this photo Dad and Mum went back to Perth for a holiday and he asked one of his staff if I could stay with him on weekends while I stayed at home all week with my Labrador, Moochie. This chap was in his mid-20s and someone you'd consider as super 'straight'. He played every sport, a ladies' man - the whole deal. On my first night with him he went to have a bath and after about ten minutes he called me into the bathroom to have a chat. He told me to sit on the toilet while he washed himself. I did think it a bit weird especially as he started to do some very provocative things. I was tempted but mostly scared. Was he trying to trick me into revealing myself? Was he a 'basher'? I held my nerve, then he got out of the bath, dried himself and we then went out to one of his friends' places to play table tennis. It was never mentioned again but was another piece of the jigsaw puzzle of my life that just didn't fit.

In 1959, I had the most wonderful sort of surprise. My sister Patsy Gaye was born on Friday, 13 November - a lucky day for us. Speaking of names, my full name is Peter Ray; my other sister is Jennifer May and then Patsy Gaye - not planned Mum told me, but I suggested to her later that she should have called Patsy, Patsy Rae and ME Peter Gay! The birth was difficult and dangerous - she had the umbilical cord wrapped around her neck - but when the tiny bundle was finally placed in Mum's arms the bond was immediate and powerful. When I first held her I knew I had a soul mate for the rest of my life. She was the most beautiful child and I used to spoil her terribly - couldn't help it. She changed all of our lives. I almost felt she was my baby and when she was about six or seven months old I took her by train to see *Auntie Mame*. About ten minutes into the film she started to wail at the top of her lungs. I tried pacing around the back of the stalls rocking her - I didn't want to miss any of the movie. In desperation I finally flew home on the train as fast as I could with an obviously starving baby. Mum was in a state. I'm sure she wished I was in another state - anywhere except Melbourne.

During this time my dad was a semi-regular on a kids' show on Channel 9 where he was known as Uncle Doug and his segment was called Cooper's Pet Corner. He was selling his company product which was some sort of anti-flea medication, or something similar. At Channel 9 I rubbed shoulders, albeit very briefly with one of the biggest names in Australian television, Graham Kennedy. He was very, very private, nothing at all like his on-screen persona. He obviously saved his kookiness for his show. His side-kick, Bert Newton, who was, and still is, extremely charming and is now a friend, was very funny on and off screen. I also met the great singer and comedienne Toni Lamond, who was Graham's and Bert's foil on the show. Often accompanying her was her young son Tony Sheldon, who was already the total performer. He would go on and be a huge star, most known for his performance in *Priscilla, Queen of the Desert* at the Palace Theatres in London and in New York.

Then dad took us back to Sydney - we were like a family of gypsies, but to tell the truth I adored the constant changes and travelling. We lived in Killara, a smart North Shore suburb and I found a position as an accounts clerk for Lep Transport, which was based in Circular Quay near the Harbour Bridge. It was boring work but it meant that I could save and eventually travel. However I only lasted about six months because one day, in total innocence, I was gay for heaven's sake, I said to one of the female staff that I thought she had 'very nice breasts' upon which she began to sob. I was hauled into the manager's office and sacked on the spot.

Mum and dad were a good-looking couple and seemed, to my sisters and me, to be reasonably happily married but dad was not a good communicator and that hurt Mum at times. Nor was dad tactile, which is probably why I still find physical closeness very difficult. He was also a true believer in 'spare the rod, spoil the child'. I experienced his fervor on numerous scary and sad occasions. I'm sure I provoked him a great deal but on one occasion I can remember serving mass and kneeling down at the altar trying desperately to hide the welts on the back of my legs. The thought of another thrashing scared me so much that I would resort to telling huge fibs. However, dad did everything else that a good parent 'should'; best schools, always well fed and dressed and, to be fair, I must have been a huge disappointment to him. Outside of the family dad did have a few 'fans'. Some of my sister's friends at the convent, who would have been about 12-years-old, used to ride their bicycles back and forwards past our home just to see Dad working in the garden. When my sister told me what they were doing, I used to do a whole floorshow showing revulsion at their taste. To be truthful, he really was a handsome man and I did feel a bit proud. Mum was also very attractive. She modeled clothes for one of the Sunday newspapers and whenever she picked me up at school somebody would always ask if she really was my Mum because she was so young and pretty.

Dad was very highly respected by his peers and for me not to be able to follow in his footsteps was a constant source of the most incredible feelings of inadequacy in so many areas. I think that I rebelled a lot because I was trying so hard to outrun his huge shadow and find a way of just being myself - whatever that was!

'Arrested' Development - Africa

In Sydney I then became a theatre orderly - not the kind of 'theatre' I preferred - at Mater Misericordiae Hospital in Crows Nest, Sydney. I do not know how I ever coped because just the smell of a hospital almost makes me faint and I hate the sight of blood. My saddest experience was when I was wheeling a very large lady in her 30s from her ward to the operating theatre and all the way she asked if I would hold her hand because she was terrified that she was going to die. I tried to reassure her that she was in the very best hands and that all would be well. I held her hand right up to the door of the operating theatre. About 90 minutes later I was called back to the theatre to wheel her to the morgue because she did, in fact, die during her procedure. We always had to have two people take a body to the mortuary for legal reasons and I was so glad because I just fell apart looking at the sheet under which lay a lovely lady with whom I had been holding hands a few hours earlier. I resigned shortly afterwards.

It was then I decided I had had enough and made the decision to really push myself and get into any aspect of 'show biz' - any way at all! Being a mad movie fan I would attend every movie I could afford and if it were a Debbie Reynolds' movie I would see it three or four times. I used to ask the distributors, Paramount, MGM etc, for 8 x 10 photographs of up-and-coming films and they always obliged. They even invited me to watch previews of their new films in their staff theatrette, which I adored because it meant I saw them well before any members of the public. My favourite at the time was, of course, *The Unsinkable Molly Brown*. I was also invited to a couple of press showings of new films where one of the stars of the movie was in attendance. The first one was *How the West Was Won* at The Plaza Cinerama Theatre and I met, briefly, Henry Fonda. He was extremely tall and towered over everyone else in the room and was so laid back that he almost seemed to be in slow motion but quietly friendly. I also met, at the launch of *2001: A Space Odyssey*, Keir Dullea, who was beyond handsome. When we were introduced my chin hit the floor and stayed there the whole time I was with him, I was more tongue-tied than usual. I saw a picture of him as he is today and he looks exactly as he did in *A Space Odyssey* near the end when he was made-up to look withered and wrinkled just before he died. Mind you, none of us look as we did 40 years ago.

My next movie theatre experience wasn't as pleasant! I had attended a morning session of a movie at the Prince Edward Theatre that had a mezzanine toilet area between Castlereagh and Elizabeth Streets in Sydney that was available for public use as well as theatre patrons. I was there to see Debbie Reynolds, of course, in *My Six Loves* and during interval I went to the toilet and began to use the urinal when suddenly a young good looking chap arrived and stood beside me and started to masturbate. To be honest I was very shocked but also I guess curious and a bit aroused so I had a look down and as I did so a second young man appeared and they both grabbed me, one each side, and practically carried me to an unmarked car and drove me to a nearby police station. I was thrown into a cell with about 20 other men, some young and obviously gay and some drunks and other assorted types. About an hour later I was then taken into an office and told I was being charged with - and I can't remember exactly with what but it was either 'being a public nuisance' or 'soliciting other males', neither of which I was doing. They asked if I had any money I could get my hands on and I told them, "Not very much." They then said I could phone my father and ask him if he could raise the money, which I did and Dad said he could. I think the shame almost killed him - not of the arrest so much, but the charges, which to him was the final nail in the coffin of my ever being a 'man's man'. To his credit he did help and I was allowed to leave the police station but had to go to a lawyer's office the following week with a couple of hundred dollars and that was the end of the matter. No appearance in court - nothing!

Highly irregular goings on! The policemen who arrested me were in those days called, and I quote from Wikipedia, 'Pretty Police; young recruits picked for their looks and stationed in the urinals for the purposes of entrapment.' I believe that practice has long since ceased in Australia although obviously not in Beverly Hills, the George Michael case comes to mind.

Not long after that we moved back to Perth and I was really tortured by the guilt of the Melbourne Tommy Steele and Sydney theatre incidents. I decided that I should seek advice from a man of the cloth, if only he had stayed in his cloth! He was a senior priest and we met at a church property. He said he could certainly advise me. He sat me down, gave me lemonade and said he would be back. He was - naked! The shock of a man of God naked with an erection was too much for me, I ran out of there and kept on running. I felt so lost and even more confused. WHY was this continually happening to me? Was I somehow inviting it? Once again, the same old question but still no answers.

To make matters worse I went straight into a similar experience with a performer I met through mutual friends. An Australian performer and a household name. I was overawed by his celebrity and flattered by his attentions but at the same time not strong enough to say 'no'. I ended up being taken back to his unit to hear some of the latest Broadway show recordings which he had imported because they were unavailable in Australia. The evening started pleasantly enough but I ended up in bed with this person using an anaesthetic cream on a portion of my body to stop any pain while he introduced me to another aspect of gay sex. It stopped the pain in that region but I can to this day still feel a very different but horrifyingly real pain whenever I think about that incident, even as I write this. It's as if my spirit was euthanised!

One night after weeks of total despair over the growing 'assaults', unable to eat or barely communicate, I decided I could cope no more. I felt totally and utterly alone - who could I possibly confide in? I cried for days, day and night. Finally, in desperation I bought a bottle of aspirin tablets and found one of dad's razors. I swallowed most of the aspirin with a bottle of sherry and proceeded to cut both wrists - thankfully the wrong way to cause any major damage. Mum found me and called an ambulance who told her not to let me sleep but to keep me walking with lots of black coffee. I can't recall much except the doctor in the hospital, once he had assessed that I was in no danger, giving me two enormous whacks across my face saying he was appalled at how selfish I was; people were in the hospital seriously ill and they had to waste time attending to my selfish self and so on. Probably all justified but I'm not sure if it's a recommended treatment for depression but it was a huge wake up call for me. A friend came to see me later and said that suicide was a 'permanent solution to a temporary problem' - which I never forgot.

I then decided to travel but couldn't afford the fare so applied for, and got, a job on a tiny Swedish cargo ship called 'Kookaburra' - yes, honestly, a Swedish ship called 'Kookaburra'.

I was a cabin boy I guess. I had to make the captain's and the crew's beds each day and also serve their meals, which consisted of a lot of pickled and raw fish! Before we had even passed Rottnest, an island 12 miles off the coast, I started to heave and heaved all the way to Beira in, what was then, Portuguese East Africa. It was supposed to have taken about three weeks but on the way the steering broke and we drifted for days. The crew, of which there were only about 12, used to get drunk at night and try to break my door down to have sex with me, luckily without success. They were fine when they were sober. I was so sick at one stage I went to the captain to beg him to get a helicopter to fly me off the bloody ship and even promised him that Dad would pay for it all - HAH! I asked to be signed off the ship in Beira but as there was no way of getting from Beira to Johannesburg where my grandmother's sister lived and then fly home I had to stay on board until we reached *Lourenço Marques*. Beira was my first overseas city and it amazed me how everything closed in the afternoon for a siesta. The crew decided they wanted to go into town and asked me along, me thinking it was to sightsee. However, they proceeded to take a taxi to a compound about 15 minutes from the city where there were several tents. The crew lined up to have sex with women in exchange for clothes - not money. It was a very long night. A couple of days later we arrived in *Lourenço Marques and I signed off the ship and prepared to fly to Johannesburg.*

My relations had a mansion with a lovely house in their back yard where their black servants lived. It was my first experience with any coloured people. They all wore uniforms and were delightful. The only time I felt a bit scared was on my second day in Johannesburg when it got very dark and started to snow, which I never imagine happening in Africa, and I was being chauffeured into the city to meet my Aunt. I was alone in the back of the huge car and all I could really see were the whites of the black chauffeur's eyes in the rear view mirror. I imagined I would be driven away, sold for slavery or some such thing and never heard of again. I was very young! I was very impressed with the way my Aunt and Uncle treated their servants - very much as family. They paid for their hospital bills, schooling etc. However, Johannesburg itself was terrifying. Theatres and shops were segregated. I found it very sad. People were being thrown out of train windows nightly and we were warned to watch out if two people walked toward you and then separated as they passed, even during the day, because that was how they robbed tourists. Needless to say I haven't been back.

On my return to Perth I really had accepted that I was probably gay but deep in my heart I desperately wanted to have children. I adored babies then and still do. I also wanted to marry because I was really afraid of being gay and what came with it. And, of course, I also wanted Dad to be proud of me and I knew that if I married he would be thrilled. So to live up to his expectations, I tried to form relationships with girls around my age, all of them total disasters. For some strange reason quite a few girls actively pursued me and the only way I could cope was to shut my eyes and go into auto pilot doing what I used to see in the movies - the poor girls!

I also tried to work in areas that were similar to Dad's business so I applied for, and obtained, a position at a firm called Wesfarmers, which provides goods and services to the Western Australian rural community and was almost identical to Elder Smiths where Dad had worked for years. I had my own office and several staff under me, which made Dad the happiest I had seen him in years. But my heart wasn't in it. In fact not one part of me was in it. I hated it with a passion. Everyone was so straight and so boring. Every second of every day was an act. I was never good at confrontation and found it impossible to go to my employer and tell them that the job was not for me, so I just stayed away and went to the movies mostly. They kept phoning home and usually spoke to Dad telling him how much they valued me as an employee and how I had a big future there, which made it even harder to explain to Dad why I couldn't stay. I told him that I couldn't go back to Wesfarmers but would try again at a firm that wasn't so 'rural'. Almost immediately I was appointed accounts clerk at a big petroleum company in the heart of Perth. Ampol Petroleum's offices were about ten storeys up in St Georges Terrace, which was the main street in the heart of the city. Why I mention that is because I had been there for a few months when the famous Meckering earthquake struck. I heard a low rumbling noise and looked at the pillars around the office which seemed to be moving, almost buckling, and I thought I was having a stroke. Did I tell you that I was a hypochondriac? The pillars, in fact the whole building, were moving and moving a lot. We were immediately evacuated. I think I was the first person on the street - bugger women first - I was gay, close enough. During my time at Ampol I tried my hardest to fulfill Dad's expectations of me by becoming involved with a woman and, as usual, screwed that up too. I became very friendly with a woman in her late 20s who let me know that she fancied me a lot - only problem, she was married but going through a very bad time in her marriage. She asked me back to her apartment in a suburb near the city and proceeded to show me how much she fancied me - clothes flying left right and centre and we ended up in her bedroom. I was in total shock and scared that she would discover I was actually gay and then all of Ampol would know. As we hit the bed we heard her front door open. I flew out of the bed, grabbed my clothes and jumped, stark naked, out of her bedroom window, which was luckily on the ground floor. After I had dressed myself in her front garden I was curious to have a peek at her husband so I went back to her kitchen window and all I will say is that I could in no way understand why she would want to leave him - he was like a Greek god.

Despite these distractions, the usual ennui descended when it came to work. The 'sickies' returned and it was off to the movies again. The last straw was when my boss was being vile to a young female staff member, really horrible, and she was in tears so I stood up and blasted him telling him he was a horrid bully and that I couldn't work in a place like this anymore, surprising him, me and everyone else. I grabbed my coat and stormed off in a fury. It worked out well because I was able to leave that job with some justification. The best thing about the job was that I made friends with, and actually fancied desperately, a fellow employee called Stan, who was/is totally straight and happily married to a lady about whom I also came to care a great deal. We are still the best of friends. Stan recently reminded me of a barbecue we had at Dad's home where Dad apparently told Stan of his disappointment that I was not more like him and that still fills me with enormous sadness.

Dad and his much loved brother, Len, and his wife Barbara spent many years touring with their four wheel drives and families - minus one - me! I tried a few times but the dust, using the bush as a toilet and the flies almost killed me. I spent most nights sitting in the van trying to pick up radio channels - anything to avoid the boredom while Dad and his brother scanned maps planning their next day's 'adventures'! Mum seemed to enjoy it as much and they did. Mum and Dad had some of their happiest times together on these journeys.

The only time I can remember any real physical contact with Dad was when I arrived home from work one day to see him sitting in a lounge chair sobbing his heart out - he had just been told that his father had died. He was absolutely devastated so I tentatively gave him a hug and he just collapsed into my arms - my shoulder was wet through. He was in such pain. Not long after, Dad had the first of his three heart attacks.

Dad and his much loved brother, Len.

Gay - Coming Out

Around this time I decided to try and stop hiding my true self and become a bit more involved in the gay scene. I had an experience at the beach and a few encounters in cinemas with knee tremblers who did arouse me a little but also scared me witless because of my previous unpleasant experiences with three people I looked up to - the minister, the actor and the manager. There were several places in Perth where a gay person could go; The Coffee Pot, The Pink Pig, Connections and a few others. No one was called 'Gay' then - we were 'Camp'. I actually joined a group in West Perth called CAMP - Campaign Against Moral Persecution - which was one of the few places we could gather safely as a group. They used to have themed barbecues which gave those who liked to 'drag up' an opportunity without any fear of ridicule. There was also Swanbourne Beach, a world famous nude beach that was an ideal spot for gays to meet for an illicit encounter. I recall being told there was chap there nicknamed 'Percy Long Prong' and whenever he walked along the beach he would leave three prints in the sand. I never did come across him! I was at the time completely guileless and quite naive. Often after a late night I would hitch a ride home. In those days, the street lights of Perth would go off about 1.00 am. One night I was happily hitching and a car pulled over and a middle-aged man offered to drive me home. I jumped into his car and we started to chat. After a short time I realised that we were not going home the way I knew so I asked what he was doing and he said that he knew a shortcut. A quarter of an hour later we ended up in the pine plantation that is now Murdoch University and he lunged at me. I asked him to please stop and just take me anywhere as long as it was out of the forest. He then accused me of knowing exactly what I was doing and wrapped his hands around my neck. In total shock I somehow managed to find the strength to extricate his hands from my neck and run as fast as I could for as long as I could, finally reaching the main road and ran home - terrified. There was nobody in the family I felt I could tell without having to offer all kinds of explanations. To this day every single time I drive past that area my blood turns cold.

After the incident with the married woman I was much more open to a gay relationship. I was attending a big ball at the Embassy Ballroom, with a girl by the way, when I caught the eye of a young trumpeter, Ray. We had a chat and arranged to meet later. We slowly initiated a relationship and I actually had my first gay kiss, but I suffered huge guilt because of my religion. I went to confession in a church where no one knew me - I used to change my voice in my own parish when I confessed 'big things' so the priest wouldn't know it was me! I expressed my fears to the priest and I have never forgotten his words: "Peter, love is often misguided but is NEVER wrong." The trumpeter, he had an enormous top lip from blowing, and I exchanged love notes and one unlucky day his Mother, who was a strict Baptist, found one of the notes - typical Keogh luck - and rushed to our place to confront Mum and Dad. The next thing the woman had us all on the floor on our knees as she prayed with both arms raised to the sky thanking God for saving us both from a future as 'poofs'! The trumpeter and I resumed our relationship the following day.

Sadly, my relationship with my father went from bad to worse. We were actually quite alike - both pig headed and VERY volatile! I can unfortunately recall vividly the most awful fight probably over some smart-arse comment I made. When it was over I looked down and in my hand was a piece of Dad's grey hair and blood. I was also very bruised and scratched but the picture of Dad's hair in my fist and the blood haunts me to this day.

I had absolutely no confidence in myself. One might even say that I was bordering on being backward in that area. I still stammered and was so self-conscious that if I was being closely watched, I would freeze - each step was as if my feet were glued to the floor. To be honest, I knew that I was 'funny' because I could think of funny things to say but was never ever able to verbalise them. I was never able to give a hint to the world of what I was feeling - ever! I was a chameleon. I was able to change almost everything about myself so that I could fit in, it was exhausting and frightening. I almost lost the ability to know just who I was!

Giving up on the attempts to become the man Dad wanted me to be, I got a job as a doorman at The Playhouse Theatre plus doing all kinds of other jobs around the theatre.

During quiet periods, I would also take temporary positions at another venue if a show needed staff. One of those events was a school holiday show at the 8000-seat Perth Entertainment Centre starring the then Jackie Immelman - now Love. They needed a follow-spot operator. I had never done it before but was up for anything. It meant a dizzying climb to a position in the roof. The spotlight was enormous and it got very hot. Every time I lowered my face to get a better view I would burn my cheek. At the end of the season it looked as though my face had been used as a human ashtray. The big production number was 'Xanadu' with about 20 performers on stage and all on roller skates! My job was to aim my spot at Jackie as she rolled all over the bloody stage singing. Occasionally, I actually picked her up but most of the time she would yell, and I mean YELL, "Mr. Follow Spot - I'm Over HERE!" My little sister Patsy was in the audience with her friends and she was dying of embarrassment.

I wanted to save money to travel overseas properly and not on a cargo ship, so I would also work from 11.00 pm to 5.00 am at a topless nightclub called The Oasis in the inner city suburb of Leederville, where all the drinks were watered down. Now that really was an experience that firmed up my status as a 'gay'. The girls would have competitions to see who could raise the most erections from the guys who would pay to dance with them. And they were not only topless, but very often bottomless too - I was numb from my top to my bottom!

I also cleaned 'rich folks' homes for a very small wage which, I guess, was why they were rich - they gave very little away. I really hated cleaning the bathrooms and especially the toilets for which the lists of instructions were often as long as two pages. If a house was especially grand I would call my sister Patsy to come over and check out all the trappings, the likes of which we had never seen before. Then we'd sit around their pool and have lunch from McDonalds pretending it was our home - talk about delusional. God I hated that job. They would leave a note with instructions and a critique of my previous week's efforts, which were usually never good enough - mind you they were probably right because I hated cleaning with a passion.

I moved back to Sydney without my parents to explore a new world. I felt freer being gay in such a big city but it wasn't as free as I believed - there were so many gay bashings. In fact a friend received serious injuries when he was bashed just walking past a gay 'beat' near St Vincent's Hospital but there were other hot spots including clubs such as Capriccio's and Jools and the saunas. The drag shows at Capriccios were world famous - so good that when Debbie Reynolds first saw one in 1978 she tried to take them to America. My favourite show was a send up of Tutankhamen called *Two Cunt Carmen*. My current partner, Sach, was a dancer at 'Caps' at that time. He was cavorting in a G-string and I can honestly still remember that night clearly.

It was well-known that the gay clubs were paying the police not to raid them and there were also the odd fires for insurance purposes. It's all a part of the history of the era now. I was also on the fringes of the first gay Mardi Gras - so many brave people - nothing extravagant but their guts and persistence against some awful odds gave us the world famous Mardi Gras of today. After we marched in one of the first parades, we were followed by police and given all kinds of warnings and a bit of name calling. To be honest, as much as I am proud of, and love, the current Mardi Gras parades, especially the 2013 parade when the gay contingent from the Armed Forces were allowed to march in uniform for the first time, I still squirm when I see groups of guys practically having full sex in the parade. I think it lowers the fun tone of the event. As much as I admire some of the beautiful bodies I don't especially want to see them 'at it' in public - save it for home or elsewhere, like the saunas

In Sydney, I had my first experience in, shall we say, a 'homosexual haunt of high humidity.' I took a friend with me because I was quite nervous and as we walked up the stairs, with heart pounding, we were given a towel, a small lap-lap that just covered our privates and a condom. I have never been one to enjoy walking around naked anywhere so I had the lap-lap wrapped tightly around me and then the towel over the lap-lap! It was very dark and I kept falling up or down steps, bumping into people who would go for a grope as they passed. My friend disappeared into one of the many cubicles with a conquest whilst I stood near the showers, one leg against the wall as I tried to look seductive - unsuccessfully. I finally found my way into the steam room. I had to climb over bodies in various states of ecstasy to reach the raised bench at the back of the steam room where the air vents, similar to those in a plane, were positioned. However, every two to three minutes I would have to wrap my mouth totally over an air vent so that I wouldn't pass out. Finally, as my vision started to blur, I decided to stagger out of the steam room. As I tiptoed to the door, it felt as though I were stepping on grapes that kept popping. I opened the door and as I looked back I could see that the 'popping grapes' were in fact used condoms! I was desperate to escape but needed to find my errant friend. So there I was, crawling on all fours, calling his name under doors or sticking my head into the steam room, all to no avail! I hurriedly dressed and waited downstairs for my friend. When he finally did emerge, he bounced down the stairs looking as if butter wouldn't melt in his mouth - other things, perhaps, but definitely not butter!

The Sydney gay scene was a revelation to me - being able to openly attend gay pubs, restaurants, coffee shops and nightclubs. I met some very grand older gay men who took me under their wing. One of them was Jewish with the wonderful Christian name of Bodo. I attended several of the Jewish feast days and was impressed by the closeness of the families and the glorious food. I attended some very exclusive private dinner parties but almost drowned in the social swim. At one dinner party I was stunned by the number of glasses and cutlery on the table but remembered Mum always saying 'start from the outside' which saved the day - a bit! Then a bowl arrived with what looked like warm water with a lemon floating in it. I thought it was clear soup but I waited until someone else made a move. They dipped their fingers in the water and then dried them on a napkin. Then the real soup arrived. I started to eat heartily despite its slightly greenish colour. When I was told it was turtle soup my stomach did loop the loops! We eventually finished the elaborate meal and the ten of us retired to the lounge area in front of a huge log fire. It was then time for after-dinner liquors, of which I had little experience. I chose the 'green one' because it looked nice. It tasted nice too, like a lime milkshake, so I drank it in one gulp and quickly accepted another several times over. The room started to spin like a top and my teeth felt like marshmallows. I asked to be excused and was shown to a bedroom where a few hours later I woke up with a splitting headache and violent nausea. In the early hours of the morning I snuck out of the house and made my sad way home. I have never had a drink of Crème de Menthe since that day!

Looking back on those years now it was a miracle that I escaped the dreaded AIDS. I was young and very excited to be free to be who I was. I had barely heard of condoms, which we called 'frangas'. In fact, at school the older kids used to meet the girls from the local convent and when they had sex they used wet nylon socks as condoms! Apart from the saunas there was a small club called Club 80, which was in a lane behind Oxford Square. It was basically a club for group sex - big groups - with a coffee bar on the ground floor and a ladder into the loft where it all happened without condoms. Just the thought of it now shocks me and amazes me how I escaped any kind if infection. Mind you, the crabs were not pleasant but it could have been so much worse.

Showbiz - Stars and Others

My partner, Sacha, was also a dancer for JC Williamson's and appeared in many of their big musicals. In fact he was in the chorus with Australia's first lady of the stage Jill Perryman when she starred as Fanny Brice in *Funny Girl*. She even named her pet 'chook' (hen) after him.

Sach and I mixed in similar circles over the years but we never officially met, However, I never forgot the cute chap with the gap in his teeth. I particularly remember seeing him at a Theatre Restaurant in a revue which I attended with my partner at the time, John Frost, now Australia's most successful theatrical producer. As Sach danced by our table I gave his bottom a pinch much to John's disgust and earned a solid slap from him. Deservedly I would have to say!

John, aka Naavil, Frost

John Frost has produced some of the biggest and most successful musicals staged in Australia, England and America, winning two Tony's in New York - one for *The King and I* - Best Revival; and one for *Hairspray* - Best New Musical. He has also produced, with great success the Australian productions of *Wicked*, the *Sound of Music*, *The King and I*, *A Funny Thing Happened on the Way to the Forum* with Geoffrey Rush, among many others, and is currently producing *Legally Blonde*, *Driving Miss Daisy* with Angela Lansbury and James Earl Jones - *South Pacific* with Teddy Tahu Rhodes and Lisa McCune and *Grease* with Bert Newton as a guest star. In 2014, John has Angela Lansbury appearing as Madame Arcati in *Blithe Spirit* in the West End. John's most recent venture in Australia was with Julie Andrews and Sacha was asked to look after her wardrobe needs in Perth. They ended up leaning on an ironing board discussing at length the wear in one of her outfits plus sitting in her dressing room, during the interval, with a coffee and cheese and having a heart to heart. He had a surreal moment looking at Maria von Trapp across an ironing board! Sacha refused payment to work with Julie because he felt it was such an honour.

John was working as a stage hand at Channel 9 when our paths first crossed. I was working at His Majesty's Theatre and wherever I went John would appear; on the bus, on the ferry, waiting outside the theatre - my own personal 'stage door Johnny'. Finally we spoke and hit it off rather well - so well, that we parted seven years later. At the time we were as poor as church mice, living on spaghetti and meatballs and varieties of canned food. We were so poor that one month we couldn't raise enough money to pay the rent, so I had to go around to the landlady's house to ask for an extension. I couldn't think of a good enough excuse so I just told her that Dad had died and I needed to fly home. Needless to say for the next few months I would phone Mum almost every day to make sure that Dad was still with us.

John and I were both very passionate and jealous. While he was working at Channel 9 one Christmas Eve, he made me promise to wait for him to come home so we could be together for Christmas morning. Of course, I thought it was so sweet of him that I refused a few other invitations and waited for John - I waited for John until after 2.00 am the next morning when he rolled home very drunk. I grabbed the nearest knife, a little bread and butter knife, and chased him down the street with neighbours laughing and yelling from their balconies, "Don't kill him Pete - Happy Christmas." On another occasion I felt John was getting a bit bored with me - hard to comprehend I know - so I told him we were going to go to Africa to visit my relatives. I didn't know how mind you and we would need all of the shots required in those days; smallpox, cholera etc and John had a reaction that nearly did him in!! His whole body changed colour and his arm was twice its normal size. Close shave for him - and me!

Speaking of size - while John was still working at Channel Nine he gained a large amount of weight so in an effort to scare him a bit I told him that when a person gains too much weight they end up breaking wind through their navel. One day as he ate his lunch in the staff canteen an ominous odour wafted it's way though the room. He hadn't heard any passing of wind noises so he assumed that it might have come from his navel. He surreptitiously put his finger into his navel and had a smell; it wasn't too good so he immediately booked himself into the staff doctor to discuss his 'problem'. Once the doctor heard John's assessment of the 'problem' he was forcibly thrown out of the office with the doctor calling him an idiot and that he was he was wasting his valuable time. I told Debbie Reynolds' PA Jenny this tale and since then she has only called John 'Naavil' - her spelling!' There was also one night when we were crossing the Sydney Harbour Bridge in peak hour in our wreck of a car, we had a huge row and John just reached over and pulled the keys out of the ignition and took off, leaving me stranded. However, he really was a joy most of the time - still is - and one of the gifts of our relationship was my getting to know his wonderful mother, Lou. I truly loved her, she was my best audience. But I did tease her. One night, I dressed up a broom as a prowler and pushed it through her bedroom window - mature stuff like that! I took Lou to Channel 10 to watch the taping of a quiz show called *Name That Tune*. During the taping there was a question for the audience to answer, they played a tune which I identified so I was hauled up on to the set to give the answer which was 'When the Red, Red Robin Comes

Bob, Bob Bobbin' Along'. Now you may not know that a lot of people who stammer find words starting with the letters B and R difficult to get out. Imagine my distress trying to quickly give the compere Tony Barber the name of the song - especially THAT bloody song. Finally, in desperation he gave me the prize - a big Teflon Casserole dish - just what I always wanted! Lou laughed all the way home and the dish lasted a couple of years until either John or I threw it at the other. I refused to watch the episode when it went to air. Lou was such a good sport and as I type this her photo sits above me.

Through John I made friends with the most wonderful woman, Mary Mackay. Mary was an Irish actress who had worked and became friends with, George Bernard Shaw. I would often visit her apartment in Kirribilli and actually sit at her feet for hours as she regaled me with the most wonderful tales of her life in the theatre - I was mesmerised and hung on to every word. Mary passed away while I was in London and John went to her funeral - well, he thought it was her funeral. He sat for the whole service but was amazed that he did not recognise a single person. He asked one of the mourners whose funeral it was and it certainly wasn't Mary's - her service was in the next chapel. Mary would have laughed so!

John then became a stage manager for the world famous Old Tote Theatre Company and we made friends with some of the biggest and most talented performers in the country. We often had drinks or barbecues at our unit for lots of those people and they were the very best parties - friends still remind us of them. People such as Jacki Weaver, two-time Academy Award nominee, would be among the crowd. She was as outrageous as I was. Other guests were famous Australian performers such as Maggie Kirkpatrick who was The Freak in the series *Prisoner* and Tina Bursill who was John's best friend, but who also became my best friend, and with her wonderful parents Aileen and Keith, very much family to me. When we first met, Tina was starring on stage with the likes of Gordon Chater, Dave Allen and Benny Hill, who had fallen madly in love with Teen, but to me he seemed a bit kinky - not gay, just kinky. Teen has also appeared in the TV series *Prisoner* and *Skyways* amongst many others. We became so close we were almost joined at the hip and had all kinds of adventures, and misadventures, some too bold to be retold here. She once took me to a nude beach in her snazzy sports car with the top down - I felt very cosmopolitan. When we arrived at the beach to my horror, she quickly disrobed, while I stayed fully clothed. I didn't know where to look, well I did and it wasn't at Teen's nude body. I'm ashamed to say that John, Teen and I occasionally resorted to a bit of pot plant pinching. If late at night we saw a nice big pot plant on someone's verandah I would drive up while Teen and John would grab the plant and run as fast as they could carrying the large pot plant while I revved up the car to make a quick getaway. I also worked for a short time for a talent agency and was even able to get a role for her Mum, Aileen, on a television series - like daughter like mother! We laughed and cried together over the years and today 40 years on John, Teen, Ail and Keith are still a constant in my life. I have been blessed with lifelong friends and I treasure each of them. The following photo is of Teen and her Mum, Aileen, who just recently passed away. I was honoured to be asked to write a tribute for her funeral.

I soon found a job as a stage manager at The Chevron Hotel Silver Spade Room in Sydney's notorious Kings Cross, for a revue called *Is Your Doctor Really Necessary?* The show certainly needed doctoring and was, in fact, being doctored right up to the opening night curtain. It was written by John Michael Howson who is a well-known writer/director in Australia. He wrote the script for the successful musical *Dusty* which was a tribute to the glorious Dusty Springfield. It was directed by James Fishburn who was one of the best directors in Sydney at that time. My favourite task every night was when one of the stars, Stephen Thomas, would do his nude scene. I would have to get down on my knees and help him remove his jock strap as he attended to his upper half. Hard job - but somebody had to do it. Stephen was not very tall but he well and truly made up for the loss of height in other areas, one of which I was blessed to be able to become quite attached to each night!

About the same time I heard about a new musical being mounted at the Metro Theatre also in Kings Cross in Sydney called *Applause* starring the legendary Hollywood star Eve Arden - who was the star of the hit television series *Our Miss Brooks*. The show was also the very first show for the supremely talented Judi Connelli. I applied for a job and all they had to offer was prop master, which I accepted. I didn't know I couldn't do it until I tried, did I? Dad was luckily in town so I begged him to help. He actually came in every night after everyone else had gone and helped me make props under the stage. He also helped build the set. I will never forget Dad's kindness because he HATED theatre. Eve was very sweet. She chatted to me about the classic movies she had made and, of course, gave me all the news on her pal Debbie Reynolds. On opening night Eve, being quite religious, gave us all a small jar of boiled sweets, not the usual bottle of wine. As it happens the show was some sort of con job and we all - Eve Arden included - ended up sitting on the floor of the foyer a few days after opening night being told no one was going to be paid because the producers had done a runner. Eve ended up paying some of the staff wages herself. However, as soon as we heard we were out of a job we all made a dash to take as many props as we could to compensate a little. I think I just ended up with some kind of a rug! It was unbelievably sad with so many people out of work - and at Christmas.

I then obtained a position as a tour guide and usher at Sydney Opera House, which was to be opened by the Queen - can you imagine my excitement? Security was extremely tight and we all felt unbelievably honoured to be there. The building was, and is, magnificent and the excitement was palpable as the countdown to the Queen's arrival started. Even though security was strict I managed to squeeze myself, wearing Opera House ID, right beside the Queen's dais. When she arrived she looked sort of pretty and pink and I could almost have touched her at one stage. Wherever she went during the couple of hours she was there, I was able to do a bit of stalking and see Her Majesty several more times at close range. Extremely exciting for me being a bit of a Royalist!

I had worked for the Old Tote Theatre Company when they toured Perth with their production of *Tis Pity She's a Whore* at the Octagon Theatre as a dresser. The week the Opera House opened the play also opened in the Drama Theatre and the person who co-designed the costumes with the famous Rose Jackson was Sacha. We didn't actually meet then but we were still constantly in the same circle. Rose was a legend in the club scene in Sydney. She had her own club and her show was in a class of its own. In fact, Rose Jackson personified 'class'. When she finally semi-retired to Perth, she and Sach renewed their friendship. Rose died last year and her likes will never be seen again. She was a very elegant and talented performer and woman.

Aida was the opening event in the Concert Hall and *War and Peace* and *Magic Flute* were the opening events in the Opera Theatre and even though I am a total 'pleb' when it comes to opera, I did thoroughly enjoy these three operas. In those first weeks at Sydney Opera House I met some wonderful people - not all stars. Some of the staff became very special friends including Edward Lloyd - he and I were on each other's insane wave length instantly. Unfortunately, we've lost touch. However, being a tour guide could be nerve wracking. I took the Vienna Boys Choir on one of my first tours. They barely spoke English, although come to think of it, neither did I. I talked a dime a dozen and thoroughly confused them.

The stars rolled through the Opera House and I was fortunate to be associated with people such as Bette Davis, tiny and frail in a wheelchair; Raymond Burr, who I discovered was gay; Peggy Lee, who was also in a wheelchair fixed with an oxygen bottle; Rod McKuen and Jim Nabors - all totally charming. Then there was Joan Sutherland, who told me to hurry up because she was freezing and I was asking too many questions. The Opera Theatre has just recently been renamed the Joan Sutherland Theatre. It was especially exciting to meet Carol Burnett, who brought her entire team from Hollywood including the hilarious, on stage and off, Tim Conway. Carol was really chatty and when she was taken on a tour of the mural at the Harbour end of the Concert Hall and was told it looked better at night, she cracked, "Don't we all dear!"

Sometimes I was drawn into productions as a 'super' - an extra. The first was in Aida for which I had to black up as if I were in *Black and White Minstrel Show*. During the very long Triumphant March scene I was supposed to be at attention holding my spear - but instead I was winking, crossing my eyes and pulling faces at the soldier facing me a few feet away, who would almost fall over laughing. I was also a 'super' in the opera *Lakme* as a soldier while Joan Sutherland sang the Bell Song - a goose-bump time - and later a matador in *Carmen*. Great costumes!

The staff uniform was very glam but the uniform trousers were, what I believe are called 'wide leg', in this case very wide leg! Running down the steps - I never walked anywhere - at the
entrance to the Opera House after my shift one night, my 'wide leg' trousers wrapped themselves around both my legs and I quite literally flew down every step and there are hundreds. I landed on my ankle but was so embarrassed I just bounced up refusing help saying I was perfectly fine as I limped onto the ferry at Circular Quay by which time my ankle was so swollen I couldn't get my shoes off for hours. But the show must go on and I was back at work the next night - full of Veganin - now replaced by Mersyndol!

I found home in the theatre. After a wonderful term at the Sydney Opera House, I moved to the new Her Majesty's Theatre in Sydney as usher, night watchman et al. The first production was *A Little Night Music* with Jill Perryman, Geraldine Turner and imported from Hollywood, Taina Elg, star of the movie *Les Girls* with Gene Kelly, who was extremely shy but had a hundred tales about her days in Hollywood and I was in raptures. We used to share a ferry home after the show each night as I pumped her for information especially about Debbie Reynolds who was a friend of Taina's. Her Majesty's was where Marlene Dietrich's career virtually finished when she lurched on to the stage, went to grab the house curtain, missed and ended up in the orchestra pit with a broken thigh. After each show she would stand on the back of a van outside the stage door and heave handfuls of her photos toward the crowd. Lauren Bacall also appeared at Her Majesty's and made no friends at all - apparently she was horrid to all backstage. I used to occasionally be the night watchman after a show. I stood guard at night during the season of *Irene* starring Australian star Julie Anthony, who also played the role at The Adelphi Theatre in London. For the whole night until dawn I would stand on stage and perform the complete show, playing Irene, of course. Thank God there was no CCTV in those days - or burglars! Then on to the newly opened Theatre Royal in Sydney where I had some of the very best times with the remarkable theatre identities Patricia and Fran Boggs and Robert Fox, who taught me so much about the front-of-house/box office side of theatre. The opening night was extremely grand, called *A Night to Remember* and starring the very popular opera singer Suzanne Steele. The only problem with the theatre was that it was built directly over the underground train lines and whenever a train passed under the seats, they almost took off with the train. I believe that sound proofing was added at a later date. We had a host of big names coming through the theatre in various productions and with varying degrees of success. People like Peter O'Toole in *Dead Eye Dicks*. His entrance to the stage each performance was a bit of a challenge for him and the audience as he took one last sip of his favourite beverage and burst onto the stage. We had huge queues at the box office after opening night - all demanding refunds! It was a total disaster and was crucified by the critics. Before it opened it had a huge build-up because it was imported lock stock and barrel from the UK (by special permission of the Union) and a big deal was made of the fact that it closed at the Theatre Royal in Birmingham and opened less than a week later in the Theatre Royal in Sydney. The whole season completely sold out before the opening night. We had no choice but to give refunds because the negative reaction was so overwhelming!

There was also a young Mel Gibson in a play called *No Names...No Pack Drill*. I was shocked at how short he was but he was stunning looking, especially when he smiled! He wasn't one to chat but was certainly always pleasant. In the play *The Bed Before Yesterday* we also had the very tragic British actress - Rachel Roberts, ex-wife of Rex Harrison, who seemed happy with her gorgeous Spanish partner and was very friendly. She gave no indication of the torment she was going through, which caused her to commit suicide not long after by taking an overdose of barbiturates with alcohol and weed killer. She apparently never had recovered from losing Rex Harrison. We also had a play called *The Pleasure of His Company*, which starred the '30s matinee idol Douglas Fairbanks Jnr and UK actor Stanley Holloway famous for his role as Alfred Doolittle in *My Fair Lady* among many other credits. Douglas was charm personified. Every female in the audience and even the usherettes fell in love with him, and he knew how to keep them all enthralled. Charmer! Stanley was everyone's favourite. He was just one of the boys, chatting to everyone from ushers to crew to fans at stage door - lovely, cuddly older gent. Richard O'Sullivan from *Man About the House* appeared in *Boeing, Boeing* and the late Robin Nedwell and Geoffrey Davies starred in *Doctor in Love*. Geoffrey was a joy. I have to say I was particularly surprised at the English performers' capacity for alcohol. I have never been a drinker and the odd occasions I did, I would end up either in bed with a migraine for days, or with someone I hardly knew! The late British comedian Derek Nimmo also appeared in *Why Not Stay For Breakfast?* for which I was, sadly, on props. The stage was a nightmare after every performance because they had a huge food fight in Act 2. Derek was a bit of a perfectionist and not much like his television persona.

One of the memorable stars who came through the Royal was the amazingly talented Liv Ullman. She was a joy, She looked about 18 off stage and wore very little make up; she didn't have to. She was starring in Chekhov's *The Bear*. I had a fling with her stylist at the time, J Roy Helland, who is now working full time with Meryl Streep and who won an Oscar for her make-up on *Iron Lady*. The relationship with Roy wasn't working out for me.

Liv would gently berate me for being 'cruel' to Roy who was one of the sweetest men I have ever known but I just didn't feel the relationship could work. The following year I was asked to New York to see her in Richard Rodger's musical *I Remember Mama on Broadway*.

It was lovely seeing Liv again and meeting her daughter, Linn. Sadly the show closed after a couple of months but the experience with Liv on Broadway has made New York and especially Broadway two of my most favourite places. Another reason I fell in love with New York was because of the kindness of a stranger. I had caught the bus from the airport and got off at Tudor City, not far from Broadway, trying to find a cheap hotel. A woman saw me looking lost and bewildered and ended up asking me to stay with her family who lived in the Village on West 16th Street. It was an unbelievable welcome to a strange new city. She also introduced me to her friend Don Grady who was one of the sons in the television series *My Three Sons* starring Fred McMurray. I was totally star struck and Don was a delight. He died last year - far too young! I also saw the opening and closing performance, which were one and the same, of the *musical Little Johnny Jones* starring Donny Osmond. His tap dancing impressed me hugely but the reviewers killed the show.

During my time at the Theatre Royal John and I were lucky to be invited to all kinds of events, some more salubrious than others. I remember going to a luncheon at which the English actor Trevor Howard was the guest speaker - well he was certainly the guest but he barely spoke because he was totally inebriated. So sad because he possessed the most magnificent voice and must have had a million tales to tell! We also saw Liza Minelli's sister, Lorna Luft, in her show at South Sydney Junior League Club. There were not many there but she was wonderful as she worked from a trunk on stage, pulling out various props. She was as good as Liza but in a different way! At the same Club we also saw Robert Goulet who was Lancelot in the Broadway musical *Camelot*. I have never seen a more butch man and his voice was equally butch, his show was excellent.

One of John's best friends was a lovely lady called Camille, who moved to America and married a chap called Chip Monck

On the way to Los Angeles I had a couple of nights in Honolulu so I went to a gay bar called Hamburger Mary's. At that time, if someone fancied you in a gay bar in America they would have the bartender leave an upturned glass on a napkin in front of you and they would point to the person who had ordered it. During the evening I actually had a couple of those glasses placed in front of me. I was drinking what I thought was scotch and Coke but in US their scotch was in fact bourbon, which doesn't really agree with me. Anyhow, later that night as I sat in the bar, I noticed a guy I quite fancied sitting on the opposite side of the bar. He was blonde, nice smile, just my type, so I raised my glass to him to say cheers and he responded. I did this a few times and nothing else happened, so I thought I would put on my glasses and sneak a better look at him - discreetly. It turned out I was looking at my own reflection in the mirror opposite. I did actually end up going home - with myself! The next morning I was so sick I spent the whole flight to LA on the toilet with a pillow on my knees and a bucket on the floor, even while we landed. The crew asked me to sign a form saying that Qantas was in no way to blame for my 'illness'. I was taken from the plane by ambulance to a hospital where I had lost so much fluid that I developed atrial fibrillation and almost died. I was given a drug called digoxin and after a few days they sent me on my wobbly way!

Hitting Los Angeles, friends in West Hollywood suggested that I use their apartment while they were away, so I gratefully accepted. The apartment was on the first floor, small but gorgeous. On the ground floor lived a couple who were in the television industry. They were friends with a lot of celebrities and asked me to join them one night for dinner with the famous crooner Johnnie Ray. I fully expected him to arrive with a chauffeur but around the corner appeared this much older version of the Johnnie I expected, rattling along on an old bicycle. Apparently he had lost his licence for drink driving. The night was pleasant to start with, with Johnnie sitting beside me, and it turned out that we had mutual friends in Sydney plus he was a friend of Debbie's. All of a sudden I felt a soft touch on my thigh and felt a hand slowly rising towards my nether region, nothing else was rising, I can assure you. I was so scared that both my legs started to go like the clappers and the whole table was rattling with them. I always find it hard to say 'no' and couldn't think of how to do it with Johnnie so I just gently put his hand back onto his own lap and feigned a migraine which they knew I suffered from, my honour was saved - well, that night anyway. I think I upset them a bit for not being more 'friendly' with Johnnie. I also didn't know that the part of West Hollywood I was staying in was called 'Boys Town' and at night if a person living there wanted someone to pop in for a bite - literally - they left their curtains open and paraded around in their jocks. Being ignorant, I was doing exactly what I always did at home when there was a knock at the door and there was a chap basically indicating that he accepted my offer. He wanted to, shall we say, 'get to know me better' and being the friendly type I, of course, asked him in for a drink. When he left the next morning I felt that I had done more than my share for Australian/US relations but from then on I made sure that my curtains were drawn every night. Honestly!

I had one other unusual experience in Los Angeles. Before I arrived, a friend in Sydney had suggested I visit a friend of his in Malibu, which I did. I drove to his small but very tasteful home, which was almost on the beach. We were having quite a pleasant evening until he asked me if I wanted to see a copy of Rob Lowe's sex tape, which I was curious about so I said OK. As things got hot on the screen, they got hotter in his lounge room. Finally, I just told him to get off me and proceeded to walk to my car only to find that he had parked his car behind mine blocking my escape. Here we go again I thought - I'm going to be raped and pillaged in beautiful Malibu! I demanded that he let me out, or else, whereupon he started to scream that I was a 'prick teaser' - whatever that is - and that I knew exactly what I was doing. Eventually, he relented and moved his car and I sped back to West Hollywood. I called my friend in Sydney and told him what had just happened. He said that his friend was a bit of a 'lech' but harmless and he truly believed that I could have handled him. I actually ended up seeing him again on my last night in LA when I was taken to dinner near Universal Studios and he was there at the table. I almost turned tail and ran but he was charm on a stick, acted as if we were best friends and gave me a huge hug when I left the restaurant. Another fun day in my life - never, ever dull!

Perth - Playhouse 'Stars' - London

When John and I separated, I moved back to Perth where I returned for a time at the now demolished Playhouse Theatre, this time in the box office which was one of the happiest times of my life. Meeting and working with the best team of directors, artists, crew, publicists etc and especially meeting a national treasure, Betty 'Box Office' Quinlan. Betty was quite naive about anything to do with any kind of drugs except those prescribed by her doctor and one night in the upstairs bar after the closing performance of a play, she and I were asked back to a member of the cast's home for a joint. Betty happily said yes but then told me how weird she thought it was for anyone to be having a roast dinner at midnight! We both very much enjoyed the evening.

There were often more dramas in the running of the place than there ever were on stage but we all went through those dramas as a united team. Threats of closure - closure - re-opening. Australia's top artists in every field worked at the Playhouse during my years there, too many to mention but to name just one - Judy Davis - who is now a huge star - starring in *Piaf*. She was outstanding though I found her to be very intense. She was from the serious school of acting; she never smiled during curtain calls, she just stayed in character. Judy would warm up before the show by singing wonderful stirring Methodist hymns. No one was supposed to go into the auditorium but sometimes my pal, Cheryl Cartlidge, who was doing publicity, used to sneak in and lie down in one of the rows and listen and in her words, "It was bloody, hair-raisingly good."

As I was in charge of front-of-house, any incidents inside the venue during a performance would require my attention. One less pleasant occasion was when I was called urgently to the stalls because an elderly woman had fainted in her seat in the centre of the row and was slowly sliding onto the floor. We had a full house so I had to crawl on all fours to her seat and drag her out by her feet - the only way. Finally, when we reached the aisle I picked her up in my arms and as I reached the foyer I heard an enormous explosion as she let go a huge passing of wind and promptly evacuated her bowels - my uniform immediately changed colour - as did I. We called an ambulance and a few days later after she had recovered she sent me a lovely note with a box of chocolates and a lottery ticket. Fringe benefits!

We had a new GM who was considered a bit of a ladies' man, in fact he was more than a bit of a ladies' man. Once again, being in charge of front-of-house my first job for the new GM was to remove a bit of this ladies' man - his semen stains - from a chaise langue in the basement of the theatre. Despite this, The Playhouse hosted many legends of theatre and I was very proud to have been a small part of their team.

One of the performers we played host to was the wonderful Google Withers. I had to paint her dressing room a bright colour at her request before she arrived. She was very much a star but nice with it. Lila Kedrova, fresh from her role in *Zorba the Greek*, could barely speak a word of English off stage but was marvelous in the play, *The Guardsman.* Tim Brooke-Taylor, the comic English actor from the television series *The Goodies* was very funny off stage. I arranged a blind date for him with my sister, Patsy, and he was smitten. Andrew Sachs who played Manuel in *Fawlty Towers* was great fun as was the tiny Prunella Scales who played Mrs. Faulty in *Fawlty Towers a*nd her brilliant husband, Timothy West. My nightmarish moment came when we were playing to full houses for *Piaf.* There were queues around the block all day. I was so busy that I stupidly asked a sweet lady who used to volunteer to do odd jobs to take the day's cash takings to the bank for me - over $5000 - which she did. An hour later she came strolling back and I asked her where the banking was and she freaked, she had left it on a park bench. She ran back immediately and miraculously it was still there. I'm such an idiot at times - a lot of times!

Later Danny La Rue hit town and I made 'friends' with his head of wardrobe and went back to London with them where I stayed for three months while they performed at the Hippodrome in Birmingham. Danny was the consummate professional and seeing a pantomime was a revelation for me. I had no idea that they were so HUGE. Two shows a day and packed to the rafters. Just after I arrived, my partner asked me to go to London to pick up his VW from his flat and drive it back to Birmingham. I caught the train back to Euston and then picked up the VW. My first time driving on a Motorway in England - at night - in a snow storm! I couldn't work the heater so I had to drive with the windows down to stop the windscreen from steaming up. When I arrived at the Hippodrome I almost needed pliers to get my hands off the steering wheel, they were frozen like a crab's claw. After the pantomime season finished I returned to Perth with the wardrobe master and back to the Playhouse.

During this time, by chance, I also became acquainted with a BBC comedy show being shown on Australian television called *Hi-de-Hi!* and was blown away by the character playing Peggy, a certain Su Pollard.

My wardrobe master 'partner' from Danny La Rue's show found employment at the Playhouse with me but I'm afraid I wasn't as kind to him as I should have been. He was not really at home in Australia and I was very much at home but to his great credit he stuck it out for almost a year and then we decided to go back to London with one of my oldest friends and her granddaughter who was about five-years-old. My friend was not only the child's grandmother but also her guardian and the plan was to enroll her in a school in England to broaden her horizons. We bought our tickets and headed to London via America. In New York, just by chance, of course, we were able to see Debbie Reynolds starring in the new musical *Woman of the Year*.

I am not a good flyer at any time but, by any standards, the flight from JFK to Heathrow was quite eventful. In the middle of the flight, a number of Hasidic Jews (I honestly thought they were called Acidic Jews, so ignorant) came wailing down from the back of the plane, past my seat and howling at the crew, rattling beads and things, trying to say something in an hysterical state, which totally put the wind up me. The flight attendants started quickly going to each window and pulling down the blinds. I took a peak out of my window and was horrified to see smoke pouring out of one of the four engines. An engine had caught fire, it was quickly extinguished but it didn't stop me from running - no, flying, up to a male attendant, grabbing him by his uniform and screaming at him, "What is happening, please tell me! I can handle it, I just need to know!" Upon which he grabbed my wrists and told me to calm down, return to my seat and sit down or else he would knock me down. I, of course, retreated. Now when I travel I take a Xanax before I board and then a Scotch and coke once the seat belt sign is turned off and if it's rough - a second Xanax. Some flights I have taken are a total blur. On one such occasion I was actually asleep before the plane had taken off and when I awoke about an hour later I opened my eyes to see that my mouth was about six inches from a young man's crotch in the seat beside me. I looked up and his face and body were frozen, with total fear etched on his face.

Unfortunately, we did not do enough research into what was required to take a child to England to stay and when we landed at Heathrow my friend and her granddaughter were locked up for almost a day until Immigration could reach the child's mother in Perth to confirm that she had not been taken to England against her will. It was finally sorted and we staggered into London, exhausted and scared. We stayed in a dismal private hotel for a couple of nights and then found another small hotel in Purley. It really was very small - there were four of us in the one room and the ceiling was so steeply pitched that we had to crawl on all fours to reach our beds. Not ideal, so we scoured the local paper and found a lovely garden flat, in Norwood. The child was enrolled easily and excitedly into the local school while my partner was extremely unhappy about the whole situation, so he returned to his family up north. I then went knocking on almost every theatre door in London looking for work, preferably in a box office. I also managed to squeeze in a few shows - the first was *Cats* at the New London Theatre where I was sitting to the far left of the auditorium with the orchestra hidden behind a curtain right near my seat. It wasn't properly closed so I could see in quite clearly and quickly caught the eye of one of the trumpeters - I seem to have a 'thing' for trumpeters - must be those lips! All during the show we kept sort of nodding and half smiling until after the curtain calls, when he indicated I should go to the stage door. When he came out we went for a drink then back to his place - this sort of thing happened several times during my life. I don't feel ashamed or proud, I was just young-ish then and in one of the most exciting cities in the world for the first time. I think the attention made me feel liked, which was much more important to me than the sex.

I was very lucky to be offered a job at the first theatre I applied to - the Palace Theatre at the intersection of Shaftesbury Avenue and Charring Cross Road. It was a smallish box office but they were a great team and also quite social. More often than not after work we would all go to a wine bar and have a really great time with lots of laughs. The show playing at the time was Andrew Lloyd Webber's *Song and Dance*, starring Marti Webb initially and then the miniature Lulu who was as cute as a button. I loved her accent and she was also extremely friendly. Most of the big stars in my experience have been so. Andrew Lloyd-Webber would often come into the box office to find out the latest figures. My first impression was how small he seemed and how untidy, bordering on dirty, he looked. Andrew kept a very close eye on figures. He knew exactly how many people were attending... who had complimentary tickets etc.

The thing that really surprised me about box offices in England was the huge amount of tickets held back from each show for scalpers, who paid for the privilege, and the proceeds were shared amongst the staff, some of whom did extremely well. There was no Internet ticketing then, tickets were like a large paper raffle book with the seat numbers on each page and a small section that was torn off and kept by the box office to balance each night. I'm sure this practice doesn't happen now and I know I never experienced it in Australian box offices, but at the time it was very common in London. During my time at the Palace I became friendly with a young box office staff member at another theatre in Charring Cross Road, and we used to have great times after work with the other staff.

In the meantime my friend and her granddaughter were settling in well. The child was very bright and loved the school and they both loved England. The weather was glorious at the time - England at its best - and people were very friendly. We did a small amount of touring. We went from Dover to Boulogne for the day and had a ball trying out our high school French. However, not long afterwards, the school contacted us and asked for the child's Immigration papers to allow her to stay at the school. We had no idea we needed them and to pursue them would have been a huge task so, sadly, they decided to return to Australia. It was heartbreaking really because it started out to be the most splendid adventure and ended so sadly.

I decided to stay because I loved everything about London - the smells, the traffic, the history but especially the people. My friendship with my box office beau was also developing into something more serious, extremely passionate yet still a lot of laughs. I also heard of a job becoming available in Claridges Hotel for Keith Prowse - a large ticketing agency. I applied for it and was told that I had the job but would have to train for a couple of weeks at the Hilton because Claridges was, and is, probably the classiest hotel in London and everyone had to be fully trained in hotel etiquette. What stunned me at the Hilton was the number of guests who seemed to float by as if they were on roller skates - they were mostly Arabs. They were very, very rich but at the same time quite friendly. I never ceased to be amazed at the number of packages they would carry back to the hotel after their many shopping expeditions. They also seemed to travel in large groups and bought many tickets - top price - to all the best shows in London. They gave huge tips and were extremely generous.

Claridges - Charges - Court

Finally I was to start work at Claridges and on my first day it was like walking on hallowed ground - once you actually got past the doorman. It was extremely formal. To me it seemed really cold, albeit very grand, with exclusive boutiques in the foyer and people who appeared to be grander than a grand piano. I was shown a few rooms and they, too, were beautiful but austere. I think I preferred the Disneyland Hotel - says a lot about me I guess. Most of the staff barely acknowledged each other but I became quite friendly with a few. Some of my clients who came to the box office were very famous and one was royalty. Audrey Meadows, the famous redhead actress from US television *Honeymooners*, was lovely. She gave me her autograph with a more-than-generous tip. The wonderful British actor Michael Hordern - very classy and chatty - and the joyously cherubic, teddy bear of a man, Roy Kinnear, exactly as the characters he played in so many movies and who died a few years later when he fell off his horse filming *The Three Musketeers*. Princess Alexandra also bought tickets - she was alone and natural.

After a few weeks of living on my own I became very homesick for Australia, so decided to go back once I had saved up some money, which was quite easy to do. I was on an excellent wage and the tips were a big bonus. Occasionally, I would even make more on tips in one day than a week's wages so it was not difficult to save. I was still seeing the other chap and it was quite serious - love letters etc. I told him I was going back to Perth and asked why he didn't come back with me because I could afford to pay his fare one way and he could then decide whether he liked Australia or not. I went to book tickets to go back via US. I knew someone who worked at a travel agency, who found me an excellent deal. I decided I would resign as soon as the flights were confirmed.

Not long afterwards I went into work on a Monday and went to pick up the previous week's takings from one of the shops in the foyer, which was where we had to leave them each night, plus the ledger in which each booking was hand written. Long story short - the takings were gone - just a little less than £4000 I believe - only the credit card swipe dockets were still there. I panicked. I asked around if anyone had seen anything untoward but no one had apparently. I didn't know how I could resign then and leave as planned because there I could foresee all kinds of dramas and accusations. I used to be the worst person in a crisis. I remember being in class at school and someone would be talking behind the teacher's back or mucking about and the teacher would turn around and ask whoever was doing it, to own up. I always felt the teacher was looking straight at me, which caused me to blush and sweat, so, of course, I was assumed to be the guilty one and punished. I didn't have the guts to say it wasn't me in case I was called a 'dobber' - and a worse punishment from the instigators then awaited me.

Back to Claridges! Almost ill with fear, I stayed at work until the end of the week, when I was able to confirm the flights and we left the following Monday for New York - our first stop on the way back to Australia. I was totally unable to communicate my situation to anyone because it looked so bad for me. The relationship wasn't working out and I just couldn't cope with the stress of the money issue. So I decided to go straight back to London and phoned a friend who also worked at Keith Prowse and told him what had happened and he quite rightly said that I should phone my employers and tell them exactly the situation. They said they understood but that they had passed the details onto the police and would I please meet my friend and a detective at the Brief Encounter bar in St Martin's Lane the next day which, of course, I agreed to do.

At the meeting with my friend and the detective I told them both what had happened. The detective said that it was serious and would I please go into the West End Central Police Station the following day to discuss the matter with his superiors. I agreed and went back to my friend's place where I spent a horribly sad and scary night. The next day I made my way to the police station and after about an hour they called me into a meeting with, I think, at least three others. Suddenly, the mood changed and they became threatening - not physically but spoke with an edge. They kept saying that they knew I had stashed the money somewhere for a later date upon which I said that I came back to sort things out not to pick up hidden money. They then gave me some milk and sandwiches and said that if I signed a form saying that I had taken the money, I would be able to fly back to Australia in a couple of days. I was so upset and angry. I refused categorically to sign the 'confession'. They removed the milk and sandwiches, took my watch and photographed and fingerprinted me. I was placed in a filthy cell with quite a lot of bloodstains on one of the walls. They gave me a rug and told me that I would be taken to Bow Street Court in the morning to be charged.

The following day, Friday, 11 June, 1982, I was taken by car to the court and placed in a cell under the courtroom for about an hour then brought upstairs where I was charged. The judge asked me if I had a permanent abode and I said no because I was on my way back to Australia. He then directed that I be taken to a police station outside of London because the next day there was going to be an anti-nuclear march through the city, where they anticipated 250,000 people to march with many arrests expected. The judge wanted me back in court on the Monday to reassess the situation. I was placed in a van with about ten very small cells - one on each side - and with a centre aisle. No handcuffs thankfully. The cell in the van was so small I couldn't stand and my knees were touching the cell in front of me. I was driven for about an hour to a police station somewhere south of London. There were six of us unloaded at the station - one cell each. The cell door was only locked at night so we were able to mix a bit during the day. The police were truly exceptional - very compassionate, with a great sense of humour and spent time with us all just chatting. The worst part was the toilets, there were no doors and the showers were ice cold. I had to shower standing in putrid water up to my ankles. For meals the police came to each of us and asked what fast food we preferred and they then went out and bought it for us from McDonalds or Burger King. My fellow 'detainees' all called me 'Aussie' and told me some amazing, often sad, stories, frequently involving prison, and the various reasons they were now in there. I was allowed to call Dad in Australia and the dear man was 100% supportive as I sobbed how sorry I was that he had to be put through this. He just said to tell the truth no matter how hard they make it and all will be resolved satisfactorily. I agreed and after I hung up I went back to my cell. They locked us in - it was a horrifying sound as the door clanged shut and the lock turned. I silently wept all night. My mattress was soaked, there was no pillow. It all seemed totally unreal and I kept expecting to wake up and find it was all a dream. It was no dream, just a total nightmare.

I want to stress how genuinely kind and caring the police were at the police station - without exception. They wished me good luck on the Monday as I was herded back into the van and locked into my cubicle and taken back to London and Bow Street Court. Once we reached the court the van was driven practically underneath the court and we were separated into different cells where after about an hour a lady arrived to tell me that because I had no funds for my own lawyer I would be given a court-appointed lawyer. After a long talk she was fairly reassuring and detailed her plan of action which surprised me because I always thought that the court-appointed lawyers didn't really put their hearts into their cases - I could not have been more wrong.

I was taken up a steep staircase that came out into a dock, where I sat with an officer to hear my charge read out. The charge included a reference to my being gay and travelling with a gay lover and supposedly using the funds from my workplace. It all reminded me a bit of a scene from an old British movie. I was in a state of shock. It was as though I was watching myself go through all the motions but it wasn't actually happening to me - but indeed it was.

The judge asked if I had a residence I could go to and I had to say I did not, so the prosecutor asked for bail to be denied because I was a flight risk - even with my passport confiscated. I didn't know how! Suddenly a person in the public gallery asked for permission to speak which was granted. He said he had on previous occasions been guarantor for people who had no abode rather than have them go to jail until their trial and he offered to do the same for me. The judge agreed as long as I signed in with the local police station three days a week and if I did anything stupid, I would go straight to jail.

I was then taken back downstairs to see my lawyer, who was so pleased for me. I was to meet her at her offices in a week's time to talk through a plan of action and she wished me well. I was given my belongings and signed out. As I left the cells into the sunlight I was like a zombie. I had no idea who this person was, what he looked like or why he would want to help me but was overwhelmed with gratitude. As I reached the street an elderly, bearded gent approached me - shook my hand and said that his name was Bill and took me into a little pub almost directly opposite the entrance to Bow Street Court where he bought me lunch and a Scotch and coke. I could barely eat and was quite emotional. He seemed kind and distinguished and he explained that he often did this for gay people who were in need of assistance - a 'Good Samaritan' for gays. I thought he was a saint sent from heaven.

We caught a train back to West Ealing where Bill lived in The Avenue, in a very nice two storey home. I barely spoke on the trip to Ealing and Bill didn't push me. I just felt lost, scared and exhausted. As we walked through the front door, he said my room was the first room on the left, where there was a mattress on the floor. Don't get me wrong - it was all very smart. At the end of the corridor was a small enclosed heated pool and spa. Bill told me to get changed and come into the pool to unwind. No pressure. I got changed but left my underpants on and walked into the room to find Bill already in the pool. I stepped in and he came over behind me and started to massage my shoulders because he said I needed to get rid of all of the stress after the last three days. I realised that Bill was naked. He told me to take off my 'undies' because they were hindering my relaxing. I did as I was told but was in despair. From frying pan to furnace! I told him to please stop because I was still too upset but stupidly said - 'perhaps later'. I guess I just knew that if I crossed him one call from him and

I was back in jail. He begrudgingly agreed and when 'later' still hadn't arrived after a few days he became a different person.

There were two others staying at his home - one of them was nice but the other, and Bill, were decidedly cool to me - not cool - ice cold! I felt like a leper and actually suggested that he send me back because I couldn't handle living like this, but he didn't make that call he just warned me that one step out of line and the call would be made. I suppose he risked being exposed if he sent me back. He then told me that I had best find work urgently because he expected me to pay rent - quite naturally.

Hi-de-Hi! and Me

In the meantime, all hell had broken out in Perth - every kind of media was reporting my arrest - newspaper, radio and television. My parents were stoic. When friends found out where I was living, I was overwhelmed with supportive messages which helped so much. I needed a job desperately, so I bought *The Stage* newspaper and saw a job for front-of-house and program sellers for Cliff Richard's season at the Apollo Victoria Theatre near Victoria Station. Luckily, I was hired on the spot, and with eight shows a week I was able to pay my rent and put money towards my food.

The shows were mostly at night and my days were free but I was scared to spend all day in the house so I went to a local Catholic school in Ealing where they took me on to direct their end-of-term production of *The Wizard of Oz*. I had the best kids - all from quite well-to-do families but most delightful. They loved my Australian accent which I didn't even know I had and were keen to be totally involved in every aspect of the production. The school gave me free rein to do as I wished so I organised for the children to make their own costumes, sets and props, which were pretty damned good. I treasure the photos taken of me with my beautiful cast - aged from nine to about 14. They literally adopted me, as did all of the staff, no one knowing about the situation I was in, of course. One of my proudest moments was after the last performance; I was called on stage and thanked by the principal, staff and parents in the audience.

The school went on vacation so I needed another job to keep me busy. I had seen an ad in *The Evening Standard* for *Hi-de-Hi!*, the stage version, at the Victoria Palace Theatre, which was opposite where I was working on Cliff Richard's show. I was a huge fan of the television show back in Perth so I was intrigued, especially by the character played by Su Pollard. After work one night I popped backstage at the Victoria Palace and asked if there was any work. I was hired on the on the spot as a stage-hand as the show was about to open. Once again every single person at the theatre was extremely friendly and they all helped restore my sagging confidence. In the meantime I kept signing on at the police station every few days, which no one I was working with had any idea about.

I was so excited to be working on a West End show. I was overawed by everything and everyone. The first person to be extraordinarily kind to me was Arthur, the stage door man, an old world gentleman who was a great pal of Elizabeth Taylor's. They had bonded during her appearance there in *Little Foxes* and he adored her. Another wonderful staff member was an adorable lady who operated the prompt side - right side - stalls bar. She had very few teeth remaining and tended to get her words confused a la Mrs. Malaprop. In between scenes during the show I had occasion to go to the bar to wait for a quick scene change and we would always have a lovely chat. One night, out of the blue, she looked at me and said, "Peter, you have come under your eyes." I nearly fainted - I couldn't recall any sexual activity earlier! What, of course, she meant to say was, "Peter, you have come-to-bed eyes!" Su said that, similarly, she was on stage with John Hanson in the musical *The Desert Song* and in a tent holding a gun aimed at John. Her line was supposed to be, "Come one step nearer and I'll fire." She actually said, "Fire one step nearer and I'll come!"

Everyone was wonderful to me especially the cast and crew. One of the crew who was particularly nice to me was Tim Redman, who was a little bit of a devil but in an endearing way. He was very proud of his sister, Amanda Redman, who is now very well known for her role in the television series, *New Tricks*. When I met her she had just won an award and was delightful. The star of *Hi-de-Hi!* was really Simon Cadell who played the holiday camp manager. He was a very distinguished actor and wasn't totally at home in such light froth as *Hi-de-Hi!*. After one funny scene when he was dressed in a particularly ridiculous costume, he came off stage and said to me, "Years of classical training to do this!" He was perfect in the role and was well loved. He later married the daughter of David Croft, one of the creators of *Hi-de-Hi!*. Simon left the show and was replaced later by David Griffin who I liked a lot. He is widely known now as Emmett, the neighbour in the television series *Keeping Up Appearances* and was one of the nicest men I had the pleasure to meet.

Ruth Madoc was Gladys Pugh - the Welsh sex kitten who lusted for the camp commander in the most hilarious fashion. She also has a glorious voice - suited to opera especially. She was a very nice lady but there was definitely an unspoken rivalry between her and my future wife. Paul Shane was Ted Bovis in the show - he died just a few weeks ago. He was a joy to be with and also the owner of a great voice. He and his late wife were especially nice to my parents when they visited. Dad thought he was terrific. Jeffrey Holland, who played Spike, was a funny, sexy man with the most wonderful smile. One of my favourites was the hyper, and continuously hilarious, Felix Bowness who played the jockey Fred Quilley. He was also the warm-up man before each television episode was taped. I never, ever, saw him angry even after he went to do a scene on stage and I had forgotten to set a box on stage for him to sit on so he had to suddenly sit 'elsewhere' on a bare stage. He carried it off beautifully, on stage and off, he was extremely forgiving of my mistake. Another person I was fortunate to meet on the *Hi-de-Hi!* set was Kenneth Connor, famous for the *Carry On* movies. Just being in his presence was a delight and an honour.

I first met Su during a rehearsal for the Ugly Bug Ball scene and even though she wasn't in costume as her character Peggy she was still very much Peggy! I expected her to be more like most funny ladies I have met off the set or stage - not funny at all without a script. However, Su is one of the funniest people I have ever met, also the most honest, intense, sensitive, exhausting, talented and very genuine. She is also very pretty when she wants to be. I've never known anyone with skin like hers, or who tans so perfectly. When she first clapped eyes on me she said, "I wouldn't mind a piece of your jumbuck!" I was flattered but mostly just intrigued. I couldn't take my eyes off her, she was all over the shop and everyone loved her. She kept saying, "Eh oop chook." Well, that's what it sounded like. I told her that in Australia a chook was a thing that laid eggs, which she thought was the funniest thing ever. Every night, between her scenes, we would wait in the side bar from where she made her entrance and I had a couple of cues to change scenes. We got to really know each other and both thought the other was the funniest person in the world. After about a week we would hold hands in the bar - just sweet and affectionate. By the way, and I'm not biased truly, every performance Su stole the show with her crazy antics as Peggy and a voice from heaven. Whenever she sang 'Look for the Silver Lining' every eye filled and the applause at the end was deafening and similarly at the curtain calls. Su also told me that she got her big break when she came second to a singing Jack Russell dog on *Opportunity Knocks*. Apparently a chap sang 'Oh What a Beautiful Morning' with the dog in his arms and when he came to certain notes the dog would let out a long howl. Su said she's convinced that the dog only howled because the chap put his finger up its bum!

Throughout this time I was able to maintain friendships with some of the staff at Cliff Richard's venue plus the new friends at *Hi-de-Hi!*. However, burning inside me was the thought that they might discover what had just happened to me with the court case and that terrified me. I really liked all of these people and it would be too much to expect them to stay friends if they knew what had happened. A true test of friendship was just around the corner.

I was having regular meetings with my legal team who were unbelievably supportive if a little tough. As an example, they'd ask me a question and if I was uncertain in my answer they would demand that I get my act together and start writing down the whole sequence of events exactly as I have done for this memoir. It was only for my own good so I would have a decent defence when the trial started. They also made their own investigation into the events. They did say that they had no serious doubts about my case, but that it would be very stressful for me, which was quite heartening. The two lawyers on my case both seemed so young yet, just as in the movies, very calm and distinguished. Of course, while all this was happening, I was still signing on regularly at the police station. As the months rolled by, they were almost welcoming whenever I popped in, and greeted me by my Christian name. It only took about three minutes to sign on, but it just felt so awful knowing why I was doing it. I also used to go to a phone box and talk to Dad in Australia regularly and he told me that he would be there for me at my trial - no matter what. I was overwhelmed. Similarly my brother-in-law, Alan, from Melbourne, was in London on business at that time and spent a considerable amount of time supporting me in various ways and made a few enquiries of his own, I believe. Their support meant the world to me.

Back in Ealing it was becoming harder and harder to face Bill and some of the other people living there, who were becoming quite aggressively rude to me. I was terrified that at any moment they would contact the police and relinquish my use of their abode. To be honest, I would almost have preferred that to the stress of the situation but I was also was very aware that Bill's acceptance of me into his home saved me from what might have been a most unpleasant experience.

Meanwhile, back at *Hi-de-Hi!* I was going through a lot of puzzling emotions, all totally new and quite foreign to me. Su and I spent lot of time all over the theatre 'pashing on' and I really liked it. These were surprising and very scary new feelings and I was certainly aroused. One day a priest of some sort caught us both 'at it' on the stairs backstage between performances and the next thing we were given a talking to by the company manager, who told us to cool it! We sort of did. I was so confused because as much as I wanted more than anything to be 'normal' - how I hate that word - my past experiences had all been pretty much exclusively gay. I even used to go to mass or at least visit Westminster Cathedral, which was not far from the theatre to pray for some kind of help - once a Catholic! Eventually, Su and I went to dinner where I laid it all out on the table - the gay past and the trial coming up. None of it fazed her - she just said that she loved me. One other small hiccup was that at the time she was heavily involved with another chap and had been so for a number of years. The company used to meet after the show most nights at the Stage Door pub across the road from the stage door where I had to hide from her partner. Once I found out that someone else was involved, we tried to cool things, but she decided that she wanted to tell him it was over. Su confided in her co-star and friend Ruth Madoc, I believe, and she was extremely supportive.

Wedding Bell Blues - Trial by Jury

Both of us wanted to be married - so at one performance, as Su was leaving the stage after the Ugly Bug Ball scene dressed in her centipede costume, I asked her to marry me. She said, "Yes!' However, Su insisted that I ask her father for his permission, so the meeting was arranged. I caught the train to her home and had the 'talk'. I was highly stressed. He was pleasantly firm but gave me a very thorough questioning. I think I acquitted myself fairly well. He was also told about the looming trial and was supportive. Next step was to book the church and tell family and friends in Australia. We also told the cast and crew from the stage show and everybody without exception was thrilled but puzzled. I also told Bill in Ealing that I was moving out and marrying - he was beyond angry. I also told the police, who arranged for me to sign in at a police station nearer to where Su and I lived, and they wished me the very best of luck! No one else knew, especially not the press, which we knew would have a field day. A friend from Perth sent a message saying, 'It must be a boy called Sue' I was marrying. Funny!

    I attended a Catholic Church in Ealing while I was staying at Bill's and booked the date - Easter Sunday. We wanted to look smart so we decided that I should wear top hat and tails while Su bought her wedding dress from Laura Ashley. As plans progressed, somehow the news leaked to an ex of mine who discovered where the church was and phoned to tell the priest that he was marrying a 'practising homosexual'! Of course he cancelled the wedding with one day's notice, so I had to quite literally run all over Ealing trying to find another church. I finally I found an Anglican minister who, after hearing my sorry tale (and I'm sure more than a little excited at the prospect of marrying the big star Su Pollard), agreed to marry us. I gave him the legal documents necessary and phoned Su, who I think wasn't all that shocked. We hurriedly phoned all of our guests saying 'change of plans' to a new church around the corner from where we had planned to marry! I think most of the guests thought it a bit of a laugh. On the night before the wedding I had a small buck's night with the best man and a couple of other friends. Up until this time I rarely drank and just twice had tried marijuana in Perth - one in a pine forest with a chap who became very amorous but I just wanted to sleep, and the second time nothing happened at all except that I was ravenous. Surprisingly, at my buck's night when they suggested I try cocaine, I did, as a total nervous novice. It just made me feel quite strange, not unpleasant but definitely strange.

The wedding day arrived and I got myself dressed in my finery in a flat owned by a very special and sweet lady teacher from the Catholic school in Ealing. My best man drove me to the church where we met the minister and I also met our guests and I then went to my pew to wait for Su's arrival. Suddenly, I felt the minister tap me on the shoulder and he asked me to please come to the back of the church where he had an important matter to discuss before the wedding could take place. I nearly fainted, what else could possibly go wrong? On reaching the back of the church from behind some bushes appeared my young sister Patsy who Su had brilliantly flown

from Perth - business class - which thrilled her, of course. It was a wonderful surprise. I returned to my seat and then the organ started The Wedding March and I turned around to see the most beautiful vision of Su looking stunning, slowly walking towards me. I just filled up to think that this wonderful woman was here for me - just for me! All during the service I kept asking Su if my nose was running, it felt as though it was, apparently a side effect of cocaine use!

We had the reception at our house in Islington, with an ice cream wedding cake, which we had to hurry up and cut because it was starting to melt. Then we took off for our honeymoon night, in an actual cottage in Swiss Cottage, via taxi. Everywhere we went

Su was recognised - waving and shouting 'Hi-de-Hi!' to everyone from the taxi. I was nervous, no, not nervous - petrified! We drank what seemed like buckets of champagne and thankfully poor Su passed out which gave me time to call two of my best friends in Perth, Cheryl and Jay, and I just shouted down the phone, "HELP!" Didn't have a clue what to do, they kindly obliged. For our first meal as man and wife, Su wanted to cook me some chips knowing how much I loved them. She poured some oil into a pot on the stove, chipped some potatoes and then put them into the pot and turned on the gas. When she served them they were like sponges of oil - I told her they were delicious!

The only hiccup was about a week later we received a call from the Registrar of Births etc. saying that because the minister had crossed out the name of the original church and replaced it with the name of his church, our marriage wasn't legal so we had to go through it all again at Islington Town Hall but this time only Su and I and a friend as a witness - the press never found out! The next day Su had to go back to rehearsals and, sadly, someone did leak the news of our wedding. The press had showed the usual respectful interest when a star marries, but all that changed when another 'supposed' ex of mine - I must have been superman to have so many 'exes' appear out of nowhere - told the press that we had had sex on a tabletop or some such thing. Of course, the press had a field day and *The Sun* had a headline saying something like 'Hi-de-Hi!' star marries 'Ho-de-Homo'. Quite a clever comment actually! Then things quietened down a little until I received notification that a trial date had been set for Southwark Crown Court and, of course, it was in the usual listings of court matters which the press found. That night I received a call at home from the *News of the World* warning me that they were using the trial news as the cover story the next day and did I want to make any comment to add to the story. I, of course, did not! We quickly rang our friends and family to warn them of the impending storm and indeed it was.

From that day on we were pursued relentlessly, absolutely unbelievable. They stormed our street - photographers with zoom lenses climbed the old church fence opposite our home and stayed there. Su had to be hidden in a costume trunk at the BBC as she arrived and left the studios. Everywhere we went they were there. The public were remarkably supportive, stopping me in the street and wishing me luck with the trial, and cards and letters, though one day I received through our front door a mock pistol with a note saying, 'To be used by Peter Keogh - on himself.' That scared me a lot. And the only other incident was when Su and I were drinking at our local gay pub, Edward VI, when a huge slab was thrown through the window narrowly missing our heads and someone yelling out 'TRAITOR!' We assumed it was because being gay and by marrying a woman I was a traitor. That was also scary and a bit sad!

Su wanted to go to Australia to meet all of her in-laws but I couldn't go because of the trial. Just before the plane landed in Perth, Su changed into her wedding gown to greet my parents, who couldn't be at the wedding. Mum loved it but Dad nearly had a stroke. Barbecues were held to greet the new Keogh family member and all, without exception, fell in love with this crazy, infectious lady. All that is, except a group of ladies who were dining at the Mediterranean Restaurant in Subiaco, where Su went for lunch with some of my friends and family. Very occasionally Su can be 'a little bit loud' and apparently she was very loud at lunch causing this table of women to ask her to be quiet. Apparently, she called them all a pack of lesbians and pulled out a breast and licked her nipple causing an immediate and lifetime banishment from the establishment.

A few days before the trial, Mum and Dad arrived to stay with us to offer their support. I will never forget their gesture, considering what I had put them through. My defence team had asked Dad if he would consider being a witness and the brave man agreed. Dad and I left the house by taxi followed by a trail of press. Arriving at Southwark Court I was taken to a room below the court to await the call to go up into the dock. Eventually I was summoned. There was the judge in all his finery and the jury all looking at me intently - I almost passed out. My heart was racing and I was sweating profusely. The judge apologised saying that because of the backlog of cases we would be sharing the court with another trial, so there might be disruptions. On the first day I was in the court for about half the day and then the other case took over. I was told to come back the next day for the expected final day of the trial. I think the worst moment that day was looking over and seeing my ex-employer sitting with my ex-lover who had a couple of his supporters with him. I only had Dad. I told Su to stay away. The press crammed the courtroom. The prosecution called only a couple of witnesses and my ex-lover, who I felt sorry for, in a way. Then I was called down and for almost 90 minutes they did their job with questions designed to bamboozle me suggesting all kinds of possible motives for taking the money, some so absurd that I saw Dad actually just half smile and shake his head. I do remember the prosecution lawyer at one stage yelling at me, "It's all a farrago of lies Mr. Keogh - a farrago of lies!" I had absolutely no idea what a 'farrago' was. We went home - press in tow - and I just passed out for hours on our bed.

The next, and final, day of the trial I kept thinking I had best pack a bag in case I was found guilty and I'd be in jail that night. One of the treasures I clung on to that morning was a note from Jill Perryman, a famous actress in Australia, reminding me that 'right is might'. And I knew that I had done none of the things they were accusing me of, so her words helped me enormously. This time it was my defence team who questioned me for about an hour, bringing out blazing love letters from my ex who claimed the whole affair was one-sided with me doing all the wooing - the letters proved differently. There were also several questions during that time from the judge. How I answered any of them still amazes me - a bit like a robot. Dad then also gave his evidence, bravely and strongly. When the judge asked the jury to retire to consider their verdict, Dad and I were allowed to go to the coffee shop with my lawyers. After about 90 minutes we were called back into a courtroom packed to the rafters. There were five different charges, all relating to stealing. The jury was called back into the court and for the first time I dared to take a decent look at them. They were all ages and I think six were men and six were women, but their faces revealed nothing of their decision. The judge asked if they had reached a verdict and the foreman said, "Yes." I was asked to stand and face the jury as the verdict was asked for each of the charges. My legs were shaking so much I had to hang onto the dock for support. As the judge asked how they found each charge, on each charge the foreman said, "Not Guilty!" The whole court broke into applause except, of course, for my accusers. A couple of the jury smiled and a couple gave me a nod and a wave.

The judge called for order and I was taken into a room to sign some forms. The prosecuting lawyer was there. He shook my hand and said. "You win some, you lose some!"

After about half an hour my lawyer said that the judge wanted to speak to me in his chambers, which was a bit irregular. Inside, he shook Dad's and my hands and said, "The jury made the right decision Mr. Keogh." Dad had tears in his eyes. I just smiled and thanked him and my lawyers, and I actually gave them both huge hugs.

Going back home in the taxi, we had about six cars following Dad and I and more photographers on motorbikes right beside the taxi windows taking flash photos. The street was blocked with press and police were called to clear a way through to our front door. All kinds of offers were being made on the spot by most of the newspapers for my story and offering a small fortune, none of which I took. Apparently our story was one of the biggest for any event in years and it continued for years! We were on the front page of every newspaper, except *The Times*, plus every television news programme. We just seemed to grab the imagination of the British public whose generosity of spirit never ceases to amaze me, but it also was a testament to the great love the public had/has for Su and her 'Peggy' character. When the trial furore had settled, Su and I decided to make discreet enquiries as to the aftermath of the case as far as Claridges and Keith Prowse were concerned. Had the police made further investigations? We actually wanted to pursue it but were advised by my legal team to let the case rest. However, I did have suspicions about a person I had spurned, probably very harshly, when I first started work at Claridges. I asked around but it was if he had disappeared off the face of the earth. Only recently I even tried to see if he was on Facebook but to no avail.

A few days after the trial, Mum, Dad and I caught a train to Edinburgh because it was one of Dad's dreams to go to Scotland. Apparently he had fallen in love with it when he saw the movie

Brigadoon, which was actually filmed on the MGM sound stage in Hollywood. Still Dad wanted to find the actual bridge and we did find one called Brigadoon that looked remarkably like the one in the movie. On the train we were only about half an hour out of London when I started to feel very strange. I became restless; my breathing was very shallow and I couldn't focus on anything for more than a few minutes. I think today it's called post-traumatic stress disorder. Looking back I'm not one bit surprised because without doubt I had just gone through the most traumatic time in my life and was able to hold myself together because I simply had to - until I got on the train. We hired a car in Edinburgh and drove to a remote and beautiful bed and breakfast for a night. We unpacked and then had drinks in their lounge with the middle-aged owners. Dad happened to see one of the newspapers on their sofa that had a huge photograph of Su and I on the front page with the headline something like 'Star's Husband Cleared'. To my total surprise Dad pointed to the paper and asked them if they had been following the case. Dad seemed pleased when they said they had. He then pointed to me and told them I was her husband. I was so embarrassed but they seemed happy to meet us and even asked me to sign the photo on the front page. Dad smiled as I did so.

Mr. & Mrs. Keogh and the Press

For about a week we drove from Edinburgh to the Lake District and a few other places all of which Mum and Dad simply loved - their first chance to unwind and become tourists. On reaching London, Su told me that the press was still relentless and, in the next breath, that we had been asked to a huge awards night at Grosvenor House. I immediately said, "No way on earth!" To be with Su's peers and many of her friends all knowing that I had just been on trial for stealing seemed totally impossible. However, Dad and Su's Dad, Don, said that it would be a true test of my character because I had been cleared, I had nothing to be ashamed of and I should just go and hold my head high. Su and I discussed it and I decided to go.

We called a taxi and set off - Su holding my hand so tightly that it was hurting but also helping. Su warned me that there were always a few of the regular press at these 'dos' to take photographs as the celebrities entered. As we neared the Grosvenor the taxi driver said that up ahead was a huge crowd of press, and I mean huge! By this time I could easily have turned around and gone home but Su said, "Chin up duck - I love you!"

As we opened the door we were mobbed, and blinded, by the number of flash bulbs going off. It took probably 15 minutes to get into the ballroom. Finally, we just grabbed each other's hand and walked heads held high into the ballroom - to a huge round of applause. Once again a testament to the great love the entertainment industry had for Su. After the speeches and awards we couldn't leave our table, even to go to the toilet, because so many of the guests came to us to offer their congratulations and support. After a few hours we left feeling very humbled and quite emotional. The next day every newspaper - except for *The Times* of course - had a page on the awards but in the middle of the page in every paper was a large photo of Su and me, her with one leg over my arm while the award winners and other guests were in smaller photos around ours. It really stunned us!

Before Dad and Mum went back to Australia, they went to visit Su's parents by bus in Sutton-on-Sea. Not to let the side down, they too made headlines on this trip when the bus they were travelling in hit the middle of the motorway and rolled over onto its side. All the windows shattered and they were lying in the bus covered in glass and baggage. There were also some pets on board and to Dad's horror, after the rescuers quickly established that no one was seriously hurt, they proceeded to rescue the animals in the bus before the passengers. Dad was almost purple with rage and said to Mum, "I can't believe that in England they think more of their bloody animals than they do of humans." They were all taken to a hospital and given a check-up and Su's Dad picked them up to go to his home. Once they got there they found out that Su's Mum, Hilda, had been sick in bed all day, so Mum made dinner for Dad, Don and herself, all the time pulling little bits of glass out of her hair. They never ever went on a bus trip anywhere ever again. Dad also was incredibly embarrassed the following week when he had to be admitted into Cromwell Hospital with very painful polyps on his nether region and Su was on the *Aspel & Co* talk show and she asked if she could send her love to her father-in-law who was in hospital with 'scallops on his bum!'

France beckoned because Mum and Dad had never been outside Australia before this trip. They were going to Paris and Rome, which we didn't have time to do with them, so Su and I took them on a day trip to Boulogne. It was quite fun, Su being stopped constantly and asked for photos and autographs; Dad directing people as they lined up to take their photos etc. The funniest incident for me, but which made Dad see red, was at a little Catholic church where Mass was being said and confessions being heard. Dad wanted to take communion but also wanted to have his confession heard first - he was a staunch Catholic! While I distracted Dad, Su popped into an empty confessional and positioned herself where the priest sits. I directed Dad to use that confessional because it was vacant. He knelt down and started to confess his 'sins' - suddenly Su opened the priest's window, pulled back the curtain and yelled, "Hi-de-Hi!' Dad!" I don't think I have ever seen him so angry - he thought it was sacrilegious and it probably was. Mum ducked for cover trying to suppress her laughter.

Before they returned to Australia I took them to one of my favourite cities, Amsterdam, for the weekend. Dad was a little stressed, and not all that well, and definitely not in the mood to be much of a tourist, plus he was also giving Mum a bit of a bad time so I decided to try and cheer him up. I had been told by friends that in Amsterdam there were lots of little coffee shops that legally served what I think were called 'space cakes' which were basically hash brownies. I knew that Dad and Mum had never seen, smoked or tasted anything remotely to do with drugs and also knew that these cookies were supposed to be harmless. So we popped into the coffee shop, and ordered three coffees and three 'cakes'. Dad tasted one and said it had a poppy seed taste which he quite liked; I told him it was ginger cake. We stayed for about an hour during which time they both had several pieces of 'cake' and more coffee. We paid our bill, a bit expensive Dad thought, and left to go back to our hotel. Suddenly, Dad grabbed Mum's hand and started whistling loud and long - he had no sense of rhythm at all so it was just the one note. He was perky as hell, cuddling Mum and almost skipping. I believe that a good night was had later on by them both. I told them the full story the next day and once again he was not happy. He said that I was being irresponsible - me! - and also that it was against the law which it actually wasn't in Amsterdam. Finally, he saw the joke and Mum still laughs about it today.

Still the press sought us out at every turn; however, I do want to stress that in all of the years we were married, especially after the trial, there were hundreds of articles published about us but none that were really nasty. Most of them focused on how we were both survivors and both a bit zany. The attitude of the press was a pleasant surprise. The only thing I didn't like was that the press knew we were 'babes in the woods' with all the notoriety, they would ask for an interview and, if it helped a project of Su's, we would agree but on condition that certain topics were not discussed. The interviewer would, of course, agree and would take us to lunch which always included a bit of alcohol, which made us both relax and usually blab about everything!

I have included a couple excerpts from articles that were in two of the biggest selling magazines in the UK which show the mostly affectionate manner in which they wrote about us, even though they both brought up all the details if my trial and even mentioned my stuttering. I'm sure this attitude by the press was one of the reasons the public were so generous to us - in many ways.

Marriage? It's - Oooooh...!

Some see them as an odd couple, yet Su Pollard and her husband Peter don't find anything odd in their two years of happy marriage...and Su's new pop career isn't doing too badly either! Brickbats in the press and threats in the post have only brought them closer together, they say. Just the day before, a reporter had knocked on Su Pollard's door and asked her husband Peter Keogh if it was true he was having an affair with another man. Not long before that, says Peter, the same thing happened to Su herself. Two years married this month, to all intents and purposes happily, yet sometimes it must seem to them that they are the only ones in the world who believe it! "We just say: 'Here we go again, doll'" says Su in her throaty voice, while Peter is philosophical.

"Well, what can you do? I guess they're doing their job. I just say it's not true as reasonably as possible. But it's always happening." It's not the sort of problem that confronts most marriages, but Su and her husband are hardly your average couple. Peter, a teacher, is famous not just because he married Su but because of a court case, hard on the heels of their honeymoon, in which he was cleared of theft charges but which revealed that he had in the past had boyfriends. It's the sort of equation that would divide less devoted or determined couples apart within months. And yet Mr and Mrs Keogh, jammed up tight together on the sofa in their North London home, insist that it's brought them closer.

"It's marvellous to see things getting better and better every day," says Su in a voice which for anyone else would be a small shout.

Peter chips in: "So often I'm just about to talk and she says the exact same word!" He's a big Australian with male model good looks and longish, high-lightened hair. He's nearly as talkative as Su, though his voice is quieter and slightly stuttery, so that it's a bit like being fired at by two machine guns, one booming and Nottingham and the other soft and Sydney. "At first it was hard for me, Su being famous," says Peter. "But not now." It seems that each has taken a small stake in the other's life. Peter acts as Su's business manager ("A supportive role," he says). She, on the other hand, offers full decibel advice on his teaching job. Over two years, and perhaps against the odds, they say they've grown together.

By Alison Macdonald
Star Interview 1986

Peter, Peggy and Potty Pollard!

It was the marriage that seemed destined to hit the rocks - daffy Su and quiet Peter. The snipers said it couldn't possibly last. But it has. Three years on they're still together, still smiling and still very much in love. And they've got great plans for the future. Five minutes was all anyone gave it, and they weren't talking about boiling eggs. Even as show business marriages go, this one seemed weighted with concrete, and all ready for the divorce lawyers to get rich on. The celebrity and the primary school teacher - it didn't seem like much of a match, more like a walkover. Su Pollard, mad Peggy of *Hi-De-Hi!* Daft, daffy, gorgeous, loveable Su and... Peter Keogh. Peter who? Ten weeks they'd known each other and then they were married. Everyone laughed. Then the troubles started and they were living with the curtains drawn, the draw bridge up. It wasn't much of a start to a marriage, hiding from the newsmen and reporters, but a very good beginning for a divorce, with him standing in the dock, his past raked over in a daily dose of headlines, while she looked pale and exhausted, as though she were about to break into a thousand pieces. And then it was over. He was in the clear; his gay past was out in the open and no longer news, but what lay ahead? We all know Su and we all know what she's like as Peggy. And, let's face it; it's hard to spot the difference. They both talk an awful lot, and they're both overflowing with energy and enthusiasm. But we don't know, and we don't see, what she's like when she's with Peter, nor what he's like and how their marriage ticks. So much has been said about him without his ever saying a word, you can't help but wonder what to expect. And then when you do see them together, you wonder just who all these stories were about. He's tall, broad and good looking and, most obvious of all, deeply in love with our Su. As she chatters on, leap frogging from one subject to another, changing conversation faster than Peggy causes chaos, he looks at her with complete warmth and affection. And she's fiercely protective of him. "Please try to leave the past and all that stuff about the trial out of it," she says. And you want to for her sake - for both of them - because they're such a happy, lively couple. But you can't because what happened in those tough, early days of their marriage had such a profound effect on their relationship.

"When all that business happened with me in court," he says, referring to when he was charged with - and cleared of - stealing £4200 to pay for a boyfriend's holiday, "it put our relationship under a lot of pressure. Afterwards I think we both felt that as we'd got through that we could handle anything life threw at us." Perhaps the most surprising aspect of the whole affair was that instead of the publicity wrecking her career, as many had expected, Su included, the upshot was the exact opposite. "The demand for her services doing personal appearances, advertising, in fact, almost anything - increased dramatically. There was a very obvious and sudden change," Peter recalls. So she'll keep appearing in front of millions and he'll be in front of 20 children. "I feel very good about going back to teaching," he says, "because the way things were going I was in danger of losing my identity, just being in Su's shadow. I have to have my own career. It doesn't matter that its low key compared with hers. Schoolteacher or window cleaner, it makes no difference, I learnt that I could never be Mr Pollard or Mr Manager. It's quite strange, and rather disconcerting, when you discover that people are only being nice to you in the hope of getting through to Su. Well, now I'm out of it and back teaching and I'm very happy to be Peter Keogh again." And just by the enthusiasm he has for being back in the classroom; you can tell he won't miss hanging around backstage one bit. The only part of teaching he doesn't enjoy is games, particularly football. "Can't stand it," he says. And Su, who's gulping down her third cup of tea in half an hour, laughs at the thought of her husband on the sports field.

"Can you imagine him in shorts chasing after a football?" As a matter of fact, yes I can. Whatever his past, there's nothing remotely limp wristed about Peter. But football, he underlines with a firm voice, is not for him. Neither is the idea of having children.

"I get quite enough of children at school. I like them very much but I don't need them at home."

Woman's Own 1987

Look out now! Here comes zany Su

Britain's funny girl swans in

By LESLIE ANDERSON

SU POLLARD, voted one of Britain's funniest women and toast of London's theatre scene, is in Perth with her Australian husband, Peter Keogh.

She popped into the Playhouse this week to meet Simon Phillips, director of the popular *Great Expectations* who is currently doing *Trumpets and Raspberries*.

Su, a fan of Dario Fo, wanted to make certain she could see the show while in WA.

Simon returned to Perth from an Australian Elizabethan Theatre Trust scholarship in London to direct *Trumpets*.

Su is on her way to Sydney as the guest of the Pied Piper Committee who will give the proceeds of their biggest fund-raising event *The Laurent Perrier Flower Ball* to the Spastic Centre of NSW.

She will be guest of honor at the $85-a-head event at the Intercontinental Hotel's James Cook Ballroom.

Asked what she was going to wear the ebullient Su said she had been given the run of his showrooms by Sydney designer Christopher Essex.

"I'm going to pick something outrageous," said Su. Her choice of clothes for a daytime outing in Perth were black satin leotards, a silver lame jacket, one earring which must have weighed a ton and spectacles which spelt "look".

First record

Her net bracelets were made of shocking pink tulle.

Su rose to fame in the top-rating television comedy series *Hi de Hi* playing Peggy, the whacky chalet maid. She then topped the bill for the West End production of *Me and My Girl*.

To coincide with her visit, Su has just released her first record in Australia entitled *You've Lost That Loving Feeling*.

She met Peter, who used to be front-of-house manager at the Playhouse, while he was in the UK two years ago. He taught during the days and was a stage-hand at night.

She left for Sydney yesterday to be the belle of the ball. Televiewers will see her on the *Ray Martin Midday Show* and *Hey*

Two Articles from Perth Newspapers

We decided also that we would send ourselves up a bit so we put a large plaque over our front door which said: 'Campus R Soles' much to the disgust of all of our parents.

They say in show business that there is 'no such thing as bad publicity' and this certainly proved true for Su - her career went through the roof. We were both on the cover of every magazine - *Woman's Own* to *Boy's Own,* which made Su a very marketable product. She was in huge demand. We were both asked to be special guests on *TV-am*, the breakfast television show with Anne Diamond and Nick Owen. Anne was a joy. She kept saying she had never met such a crazy pair. When I look at the clip now, and I haven't for years, I almost vomit. I talked like a thrashing machine and at one stage got a bit giggly - horrible to watch now! Su was on every television talk show - *Sunday, Sunday* with Gloria Hunniford, who became a friend, Joan Rivers, who adored Su, Gay Byrne's show in Ireland, Michael Parkinson, who would chat to me about his family in Australia, Richard and Judy, (I always thought he seemed a bit gay but he totally was not), Russell Harty, very camp and very nice, Val Doonican, who was the sweetest man, England's Perry Como. Dad really loved a duet he filmed with Su, 'Can't Get Used to Losing You'. *Pebble Mill at One,* Kenny Everett, wonderfully outrageous - he had a sister living in Perth, and *Noel's House Party* with Noel Edmonds among many others.

Another memorable, if unnerving experience, was when Oliver Reed threw his beer near Su on the infamous episode of *Aspel & Co*. On the night of the show we arrived at the studio and were greeted by the publicity people, who took us to the Green Room to meet the other guests. I can recall Clive James being there, a lovely friendly Aussie, and snooker champion Steve Davis, who was a bit shy but no one else. As the show progressed I watched from the audience and all was fun until an absolutely sozzled Oliver Reed appeared carrying a drink and started in on Aspel and the other guests, but especially Su. He was so rude to her but she handled it with great aplomb, although I could see her turning bright red, not a good sign! Later, in the Green Room I was so furious I refused to meet him but chatted with Clive and Steve and then Michael came over and apologised for Oliver and congratulated Su on her professionalism. It made headlines everywhere - even in Australia.

On another occasion the English *Woman's Own* flew us both to Bali to do a photo shoot to accompany a big piece they were doing on us - not hard to take! We were also flown to New Zealand for their big Telethon where Su is as popular as she is in the UK. We landed in Wellington where we were treated like royalty, which really shocked and pleasantly surprised us. We spent half a day reading out donations and some of those Maori names were a challenge. Su was hilarious trying to pronounce them. Also in New Zealand was Estelle Getty from the *Golden Girls*. We had a snack with her and her gay son and she was nothing like the Mother she played in the show - much, much prettier and so tiny! At the conclusion of Telethon, the producers were so impressed by the extra effort Su (and me I suppose) put in that they flew us to Sydney for a holiday before returning to London.

Following are a few of the shots from the many photo shoots requested by the media!

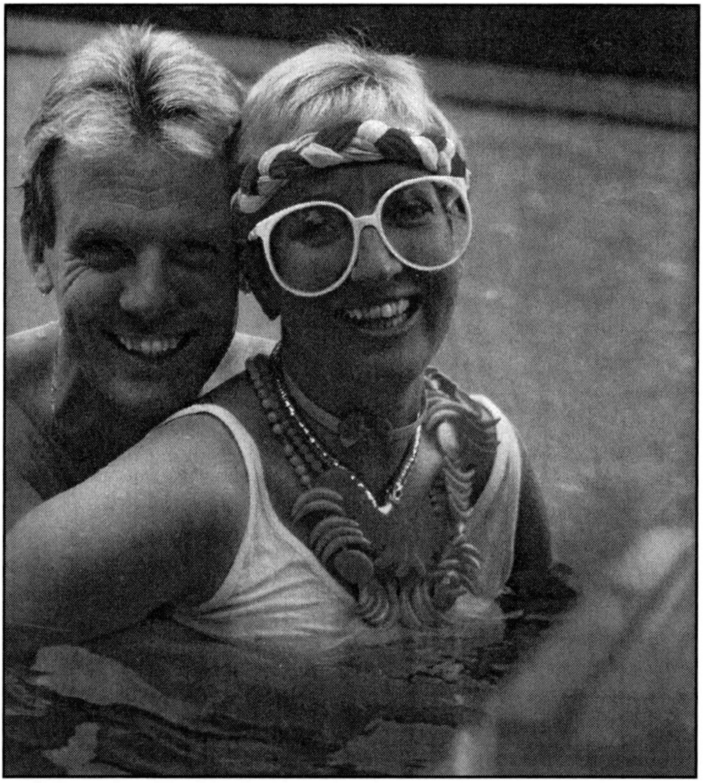

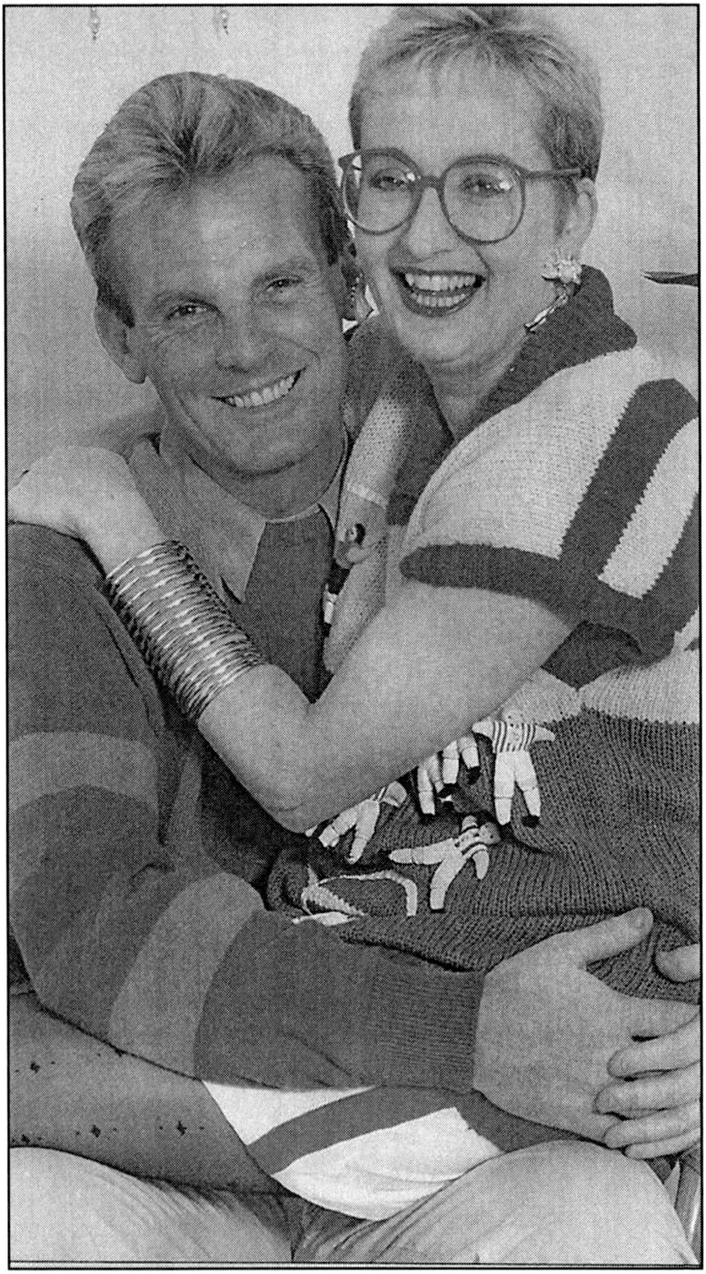

Earlier, I mentioned that I was a hypochondriac, well to be more accurate, HYPOCHONDRIAC. As I had 'been around' I wanted an AIDS test regularly because I read that one could carry the virus for years and even though I had not had gay sex for years I insisted on the tests. Finally, our doctor lost the plot and almost screamed, "Enough with the AIDS tests," and so I finally stopped. Speaking of AIDS, Su used to go to hospices regularly to meet and talk to AIDS patients in their final stages and give them the support and hugs they longed for.

One incident relating to my hypochondria was quite funny. Su was on tour and I was in our bed sound asleep when a noise woke me up. To my horror I found that my left arm was totally numb, as if it were someone else's arm on my body. My whole left side felt 'strange' and I was convinced that I was having a stroke. We kept the telephone in our wardrobe to muffle the ringing so I dragged myself onto the floor and into the wardrobe to dial emergency. The ambulance arrived in minutes and as our bedroom was on the second floor with the steepest, narrowest staircase they couldn't use a stretcher so they had to tie me into a chair to carry me down to the ambulance. The hospital was about 15 minutes away and after about five minutes my arm etc. began to feel normal. It was then I realised had I had just gone to sleep with my arm folded under my head, nothing more than that! I told the paramedics who laughed, did a few quick tests and agreed to take me home - only asking for a signed photo of Su when she returned.

Married Life - Princess Diana and 'Others'

I used to love attending the location filming and later the studio filming of *Hi-de-Hi!* at the BBC Shepherd's Bush studios. We stayed at the Cliff Hotel in Dovercourt, Essex, which was alongside the camp where they filmed. In the middle of the night, Su would run down the corridors knocking on doors and hiding and also mixing up all of the shoes waiting to be cleaned. However the staff adored her. There was also a parrot that Su desperately tried to teach how to swear. When any of my family visited from Australia one of the highlights of their trip was attending the filming and taping as VIP guests. During the taping back in London, the audience would go crazy when they introduced Su and the other performers but - and I may be biased - especially Su. Felix, the warm-up man, always introduced me as 'Su's old man' which I loved. As well as being Su's husband I was her biggest fan and a huge admirer of the many talents she has. After each taping at the BBC studios a big thank you reception was held in their Green Room for all the cast and crew where they showed the hilarious out-takes which I especially enjoyed. After the final *Hi-de-Hi!* I really wanted Su to be a bit more outgoing in promoting her many talents. She would always ask my advice on every aspect of her career and as the publicity machine stayed in high gear it was a perfect opportunity to broaden her career. The very last episode was such a tearjerker and it mainly featured Su as Peggy finally winning her Yellow Coat. It was brilliantly written and directed and, of course, acted and was also a huge rating success - repeated over and over for months.

In the meantime, we were both asked to attend all kinds of social functions as a couple - opening fetes, appearing at gay pubs and clubs etc. We appeared in the London Lord Mayor's Parade, ran the local marathon - well the last one hundred yards and then I supposedly fainted in Su's arms - another front page shot! Su also never forgot her gay fans who were one of the reasons she was so popular - they loved her. We used to go to a little gay pub where the owner was a gay English chap who was a little dark skinned. Su always called him 'Mrs. Ghandi' to his face, which he loved. It was impossible to take offence with Su except, of course, the ladies who lunched at the Mediterranean Restaurant back in Perth!

A disturbing and, I guess, oddly flattering matter was the number of people who were still coming out of the woodwork saying that they had had sex with me. When cornered, it came out that it happened in places where I had never been, or when Su and I were out of the country. I can recall a gay friend I really cared about who was part of a small group of people I mixed with, especially when Su was touring, getting quite angry with me and when I asked what the matter was he said that one of the group had told him that he had had sex with me! Nothing I could say would convince him. I should have asked these people to describe my private parts in detail, which they obviously could not. It was so frustrating. Equally surprising to both Su and I was the occasional straight man who would corner me at an event to ask me all kinds of questions about being gay. Every now and then I would have some man shake my hand and in the palm of his hand was a piece of paper with their name and phone number. I thought it rather unusual but we both also thought it weirdly flattering. At our home one day, a very passionate note was pushed through our door addressed to Su Pollard's husband - they didn't even know my name - not quite so flattering!

Su had fans who sometimes surprised us, one of these being Cardinal Hume, who invited her to dinner at Archbishop's house where during the evening the Cardinal told Su that he was also a huge fan of the Gladys Pugh character played by Ruth Madoc in *Hi-de-Hi!* and proceeded to do a quick impression of her. Su was delighted. She also often received fan mail from staff at

Buckingham Place who were mostly gay it seemed, at least her fans were, and they would follow her career closely and loyally.

We also were invited to many opening nights of musicals, plays and movies and also celebrity lunches and launches. One memorable occasion was the musical *Sugar Babies*, which opened at the Savoy Theatre starring Hollywood legends Ann Miller and Mickey Rooney and co-starring the Australian actress Rhonda Burchmore. When we met backstage Rhonda was having a joke with her guests by having steel wool protruding from her costume - representing pubic hair - very much the raunchy sense of humour Su enjoyed! It was a fun show and afterwards we were invited to dinner with Ms Miller and her party. She was in her late 60s but had almost waist-length jet black hair pulled straight back off her face and the most amazing figure. Being the complete Hollywood groupie, I barely spoke, but Su rattled on at her for a long time and as I was watching I saw Ms Miller's eyes glaze over, her Hollywood smile frozen. She had no idea who Su was or what she was saying but she remained very gracious! We also attended a luncheon to launch Jane Russell's new book. Jane was very tall and she looked as if she had lived a very full life - and without meaning to be too unkind, she did look a little like a man in drag. I think we said about ten words to her as she signed her book. We sat beside the actor Robert Powell who had just finished filming in Perth with my friend, the aforementioned Mary Mackay, which was a great conversation opener - his eyes were as mesmerising as was his voice. We also met Barbara Windsor a few times. I sat beside her one evening in a very grand marquee for a glamorous dinner and I told her she reminded me a little bit of Debbie Reynolds, mainly because they were both so petite. She feigned modesty and was pleasant but I could tell that she was not all that thrilled because Su was definitely the flavour of the month. However, now Barbara is a 'living legend' with a Queen's honour, but I found her to be very aware of every move she made and not naturally warm or funny! Another lady I met briefly and adored at the BBC was Joanna Lumley - she looked exquisite, spoke beautifully and was deliciously funny. She called Su 'Polly' because they went back quite a long way together. I was also thrilled to meet and chat with Joan Sims from the *Carry On* movies. She was older, certainly, but a joy to be with. When I told her that I had loved her since I was 15 she became quite teary. On another occasion, because Dad was a huge admirer of Margaret Thatcher, when Su was invited to 10 Downing Street - this time without me - she asked Mrs. Thatcher for her autograph for her father-in-law, which she immediately handed to Su. Dad was thrilled. One observation I did make was that Su was not popular with the more sophisticated type of comediennes at the time, but she was the only one who was as naturally funny off stage as she was onstage.

We were also thrilled to attend two functions where the special guest was Princess Diana. The first was a luncheon at the Savoy not long after she returned from Australia. We sat beside Maureen Lipman and I could hardly eat I was laughing so much - I had no idea that she was so damned funny. After lunch, when the Princess moved over to our little group, she looked a bit tired. I asked her how she enjoyed Australia - she said, "Oh yes, you're Australian aren't you? All I can really remember is the heat and flowers." The second occasion was not long after and was a much smaller function in a room off the side of Westminster Abbey. Su was dressed in the most amazing three quarter length dress that looked as though it had been knitted with huge knitting needles and was every colour. Diana came to us and said, "We meet again so soon - Su you are definitely our rainbow girl - I adore your dress." She chatted for at least ten minutes mainly about her sons because it was a 'thank you' event for people who had worked on a charity for sick kids, which Su had been doing.

I then started to assist at another Catholic school in Islington, St John the Evangelist, which I adored. I made friends with people I still see and stay in contact with today - Paul Callaghan and Sally Brookes especially. I hadn't been there long when a couple of the parents heard about me being there and came to the school gate with a sign saying, "Get rid of the homosexual!" I was devastated and went to see the headmistress, a sweet nun who knew, along with the rest of the staff, about my trial. I told her I would leave and she said she wouldn't hear of it because she valued my contribution hugely. All of the staff concurred which really touched me. I have to say, that behind the scenes at a school can sometimes make behind the scenes in theatre quite tame. None of the children knew that I was married to a huge star until I brought Su to a school function - they were gob-smacked. Su was very generous of her time at the school; she would open the fetes and attend all kinds of school events as Mrs. Keogh, which made me very proud.

It was soon our first anniversary, which we decided to celebrate at the school church with the cast of *Oliver*, the school musical Paul and I were co-directing - singing some beautiful music during the service. One of the parish priests was Monsignor Bruce Kent, who was very controversially active for CND - the Campaign for Nuclear Disarmament, and he officiated at the half hour service. He has since left the priesthood and married - a woman. Su wore her wedding dress and the reception was held in the school assembly hall, where once again the children sang for us, this time songs from *Oliver*. Su also sang 'All of Me', which was a knockout. Su told me that she once sang that song at an audition and when she had finished the director said, "No thank you Miss Pollard - we don't want any of you." The brilliantly talented and wonderful Fay Presto donated her time as a gift to us and delighted us all with her unbelievable magic. I have learned that Fay has been voted The Magic Circle Close-up Magician of the Year 2012 - well deserved. Amongst the many guests were a lot of the cast of *Hi-de-Hi!* and also the two lawyers who defended me in court, plus one of the psychologists who supported me through some very bad and sad times - Frances Drummond. The next day - all over the newspapers again - full page photos and articles.

During this time I also met Su's adorable Auntie Elsie. No matter what was said to her she usually replied, "That's the main thing!" One time we told her that a friend had died and she just looked straight at us, smiled and said, "That's the main thing!"

In some ways, our lives were full of parties and celebrities, but we both tried to do our share helping others less fortunate than us; me in a small way with my Boy's Club work and Su with her many charities. One in particular still shocks me today. Su was asked to do a Community Service announcement for people unable to afford their power bills as we lived through one of the most severe winters on record. In the announcement she told these people that the best way to conserve their body heat was to get into a large plastic bin bag, pull it up to their neck and tuck it into their top. Every time I turn a heater on since then I feel a sense of guilt.

There were some wonderful fringe benefits from being married to a big star. Su was asked to perform her cabaret act on a QE2 Mediterranean cruise - a fellow celebrity guest was Gloria Hunniford who was with her partner at the time and her son Michael Keating. Gloria is definitely one the nicest women I have ever met anywhere. We all got on so well on the cruise and Gloria and Su became firm friends. I spent some time with her son, Michael, who had the most delightful and mature sense of humour for a person so young. When it was Su's night to present her show, I helped her set up and rehearse but while her show was on I just went out onto the open deck and lay flat on my back until I could hear the cheering as she finished the show - I am the world's worst worrier. Also on the cruise were 'Agony Aunt' Claire Rayner and her husband, Desmond. She was a very jovial lady - everyone's friend.

West End - 'Me and My Girl'

Sydney was my chance to show Su off to friends on the other side of Australia including my ex, John Frost, who liked her a lot. When they knew we were coming, a friend, 'Lady' Olga Byron, who worked at Channel 9, arranged for Su to be a special guest on the top-rating *Midday Show* to sing and chat. Much excitement ensued. The day arrived and Su had a great rehearsal of her number, 'Let's Hear it for Me', with the big band conducted by Geoff Harvey. The regular host, Ray Martin, was off and a very straight-ish news reporter called George Negus was his replacement. Su was wearing a short, lemon-coloured dress. After the song she joined George for the chat. Several times during the interview, Su would swivel in her chair and cross and uncross her legs quickly - she was always a bit hyper - someone once said that she was like a 'bee on speed'. Whenever she did this I heard loud guffaws from the cameramen and found out later that she had no panties on and whenever she crossed and uncrossed her legs her 'map of Tasmania' was on display for all to see - a first for Aussie TV and that too made the news. Lady Olga told me that the crew at their Christmas parties always showed a gag reel and their favourite that year was Su's 'map' which they kept freezing in certain positions!

Also in Sydney, Su met my best friend, Tina Bursill, and her parents, Aileen and Keith, and they immediately fell in love with each other. Ail and Su both enjoyed a drink of which they partook in several over lunch at the Mosman Rowing Club, built over the water on Sydney Harbour. It was the home of some of the world's most dangerous sharks! It was a sweltering day so after lunch Ail and Su both wanted a swim. We just laughed and told them not to be silly, which was like a red rag to a bull. Suddenly they stood up, walked to the outside deck, stripped to bras and pants and

dived in, as we screamed like banshees. We grabbed their clothes and ran to the shore to hopefully meet them. I know that they were legless when they entered the water but I didn't want them literally legless as we hauled them from the harbour! Luckily it must have been an off day for sharks. Ail and Su staggered out of the water friends for life!

Sydney was the best time. Everywhere we went, Su was recognised and we couldn't go too far before she was signing autographs, posing for photographs and chatting to fans. All of my friends made Su most welcome - practically adopted her - special friends like Kathy and Steve Bocksette, who now live in Perth. John Frost organised for us to attend some shows and we had dinner at the place I once shared with him, still with dents in the walls from us throwing things at each other. John also arranged a horse-riding party with friends north of Sydney on a rather large property, with lots of rather large horses. It was Su's first time in a saddle, on a horse at least, and she was a tad nervous, mind you, so was I. John had arranged for Su to have a gentle horse and we cautiously waddled off around the property. After about half an hour Su heard John yell to someone, "Hurry up and get a vet!"

Whereupon she absolutely panicked, demanding to know, "Why the fuck do we need a vet?" However, she was mollified when it was explained to her that what John had actually said was 'Hurry up and get Yvette!'

The following year we were again flown back to Sydney where Su was the star guest at one of the biggest social events of the year at The Intercontinental Hotel where we were also staying. When we checked in, to our surprise, we were taken to the biggest suite in the hotel. Oprah Winfrey recently stayed in the exact room. It occupied almost a whole floor with views of the harbour, Opera House and around to the city. When the manager left us in the suite, we dropped our bags and ran into every room - jumped on the beds and hugged each other, dancing around the suite - babes in the VIP Suite. Su never took anything for granted and lovely gestures such as being given the suite really excited her - and me!

At the Intercontinental Ball in Sydney

On yet another occasion we were flown with a plethora of famous people to Liverpool of all places on Concorde to attend the Grand National horse race, my first ever horse race and my first and last trip on Concorde. It was very much like a long thin tube and I could just stand without my head touching the ceiling. They flew us around as we drank champagne and were then given a tour - two at a time - of the minute cockpit. Su being Su started to touch things which made the pilot and crew quite nervous. They told her to please desist because it was very dangerous. It was said with a smile and a bit of a shocked expression.

When we returned to London, Su was offered the role of Sally, the 'Girl' in the hit musical *Me and My Girl* in the West End at the Adelphi Theatre on the Strand, taking over from Emma Thompson. She wasn't going to do it because she had no confidence in herself as a dancer and the role required a lot of dancing, including tap. I kept trying to instil some confidence in her abilities and quickly accepted when the director Mike Ockrent asked us to his home for lunch. He and I both hoped that by having a relaxed chat with him and also the choreographer, Gillian Gregory, Su might change her mind and indeed she did. She used to struggle to dance rehearsal every day for a few weeks before the main rehearsals started and she would almost crawl home with tap shoes in hand, completely exhausted but she didn't give up. Her co-stars were Enn Reitel, the funniest man who could 'do' all kinds of voices; Frank Thornton, from *Are You Being Served?* - a lovely gentleman; Ursula Smith, terribly grand but an absolute joy; and Su's understudy, the Australian actress Caroline O'Connor, who is now a big star in Australia and Broadway. Opening night was one of my proudest. All the hard work came together beautifully and Su was brilliant - touching and funny - her voice filling the Adelphi Theatre, and yes, she got through the dances quite well. Dad was still in hospital but Mum was there glowing, meeting all the guests and falling in love with John Inman, also from *Are You Being Served?*

WEEKEND

27p (R. of I. 44p) JANUARY 16-22, 1985

EXCLUSIVE INTERVIEW

Prince Philip talks to Weekend

As always...
Controversial
Hard-hitting
To the point

CRAZY MAN – BY
U POLLARD

Winter coats for under £60

OUR WORLD
SU POLLARD
AND PETER KEOGH

They're the craziest pair in showbiz — she's crazy about him and he's crazy about her! Maggie Henderson went to meet a couple who are Hi on life...

Su Pollard

For comedienne and singer Su Pollard of 'Hi-de-Hi!' fame (above), December 25 is enhanced by her Australian school teacher husband's wonder at it. 'At home Christmas dinner is salad and snow is squirted on the windows by aerosol,' says Peter Keogh. 'Here you get the real stuff.' This year they're looking forward to their fifth British Christmas together, which Su defines like this:

Crucial kick off
'Peter has always gone to Midnight Mass on Christmas Eve wherever he has been in the world. Now I go with him after the pantomime (this year Su's in *Dick Whittington* at Richmond Theatre from December 15 to February 7 with Christmas Day off) and it's the perfect start.'

Childhood legacy
'We both have to have a stocking with an apple, orange and fifty pence in it to open first thing.'

Tree lore
'Real, definitely. We had a fake one but when we got it out of the cubby hole its leaves were all bent, it was nearly naked.'

Trimmings
'I'm obsessed by gold bells, which I stick on the ceiling with double-sided tape. And I love Chinese lanterns.'

Presents
'Usually we set a five pounds limit and pile them all round the tree for opening when family and friends arrive. Last year I managed to find a sort of Dinky car with built-in radio, also a miniature office stationery set with letter opener, paperclips and so on.'

Memories
'When I was about two, I had this wonderful doll and my sister sat on its head on Boxing Day. She couldn't help it but it was very tragic.'

Essential tryst
'Switching on for the Queen. We're all nosy, aren't we, and I love watching her speak from her own house.'

Telling taste
'Knobbies! That's what we call sprouts in Nottingham where I come from. Sprinkled with lemon juice, a dash of sugar and butter, they're lovely. Also I'm a sauce queen. With the bird, I love piccalilli, red cabbage, cranberry sauce, onions *and* the smell of mustard going up my nose.'

Teatime treat
'Smoked salmon sandwiches.'

Party pieces
'I've been doing *Won't You Come Home Bill Bailey?* since I was fourteen and one year in Australia, visiting Peter's parents, my mum, who's pretty quiet, did *You Made Me Love You*. But nothing from Peter, he's not like that.'

Emotional moment
'If I don't have a good cry on Christmas Day, then it's not right. It's the thought of everybody joined in goodwill and being nice to each other that does it. Even the carols make me cry.'

Different this year
'Peter will be wearing a suit and tie! My parents will be in Australia, I'll be working hard so for the first time we're going out to a restaurant with friends. We'll both miss the family a lot, the telephone will be on overtime.'

Postscript
'If you're reading this, Vena I love those home-pickled onions you give me, even though I did once eat a whole jar to myself and got acid stomach!'

Top of the Pops - 'Starting Together'

Su was also very active in other areas at this time, including recording the theme song for a new BBC documentary series called *The Marriage*, which was produced by Desmond Wilcox, the husband of Esther Rantzen. After she had recorded the song we all just basically forgot about it but that soon changed once the series was aired. Suddenly it was the top-rating show on television and the BBC was inundated with requests for the song to be released as a single. It was called 'Starting Together' and written by Bill Buckley. It was eventually released and went to No. 2 on all of the music charts where it stayed for weeks. Only Diana Ross's song 'Chain Reaction' kept Su from being No. 1. I was then able to convince her to make more recordings and eventually an album, all of which did rather well.

I have to say that our life wasn't always hearts and flowers - to use the name of Su's book - sometimes it was *Hearts and Showers*. We were both very volatile and hyper people and when we got angry we got very angry but, I must say, not very often. One awful time was the day Su was to appear on a Royal Variety type show at the National Theatre where Princess Anne was the guest. Su was singing 'The Lady is a Tramp' from the show she was touring with, *Babes in Arms*, co-starring the irrepressible Matthew Kelly. About two hours before we were to leave for the theatre we had a terrible fight, terrible because it was the only time we actually became physically angry. I honestly can't recall what it was over but Su lunged at my face and her nails cut open the bridge of my nose, then she jumped on my back, so to get her off I bent over and she went hand first into a glass door. There was blood everywhere - my nose and her hand. I called an ambulance because the cut on her hand looked quite deep. They arrived in minutes and on walking in, seeing it was Su Pollard, immediately asked for her autograph before doing anything else. The cut was deep and it was heavily bandaged so that she could perform on the show in about an hour or so. On the tape of the show you can easily see her hand and the bandages - not my proudest moment. Su still has small scar on her hand and I have a small one on my nose - war wounds! The only other time we had serious words, but no violence, was when I was giving the house a quick clean and in the bathroom I saw little bits of what looked like cat poop around the base of the toilet bowl so I wrapped my hand in toilet paper and cursing the cats, picked it up and flushed it down the toilet. It turned out to be something that Su would very occasionally smoke to help her relax and it was worth a considerable amount of money!

At another Royal Event - I think it was *A Night of 100 Stars* at the Dominion Theatre, Tottenham Court Road - Su was on the bill and I was arriving late after school with my best friend, Paul, to see the show. As we entered the foyer dressed in work clothes, we were bustled into a line of people. We had no idea what was happening so we just did as we were told. Suddenly Princess Margaret appeared and we were actually in her welcoming line-up - hilarious timing. As Su finished her song, 'Let's Hear it for Me', which was the last act before interval, the applause was long and sustained. Paul and I had no doubt Su had stolen the show, especially after listening to the feedback from the audience who were comparing her to Barbra Streisand.

Su appeared in many Royal Variety Shows but the one I most remember was held at the Theatre Royal Drury Lane in 1986. Being the husband of a performer I was allowed backstage during the rehearsal. I most remember being in the wings as Paul McCartney was rehearsing and as he passed me he just smiled and said 'Hi' but his then wife, Linda, stayed in the wings with me for over half an hour as they did sound checks and she was one of the nicest people I have ever met in the business we call 'show'. She was quite beautiful and was as interested in what I was doing as I was in her and Paul. She also told me that they very much enjoyed *Hi-de-Hi!* It was such a sad loss when she died so young.

At the after-show party, which we were almost the last to leave, I met one of my idols - the beautiful actress Jean Simmons, who was also in the show. I told her the usual fan stuff - how I loved her work in *Spartacus*, *Guys and Dolls* etc, but that I most enjoyed her work in the Debbie Reynolds, Dick van Dyke movie, *Divorce American Style* and then she really opened up and told me that it was one of her favourite movies too and she was surprised that I even knew of it. We had the best chat and she looked amazing - she had the deepest green eyes that have been called 'snake charmer eyes'.

Following is a list of some of the stars who appeared in *The Royal Variety Show* that year. I was able to meet and even chat to a lot of them - how lucky can a star-struck boy from Perth be?

Compere: Peter Ustinov

SHARON GLESS, PETULA CLARK, RORY BREMNER, PEKING OPERA, VICTORIA WOOD, STEPHANE GRAPPELLI, NANA MOUSKOURI, VICTOR BORGE, FRANK CARSON, TYNE DALY, KEN DODD, HUDDERSFIELD CHORAL SOCIETY, VAL DOONICAN, GLORIA HUNNIFORD, ALED JONES, BOB MONKHOUSE, SU POLLARD AND RUTH MADOC, LULU, RONNIE CORBETT, PAUL McCARTNEY, PAUL NICHOLAS, NICHOLAS PARSONS, PAUL DANIELS

On another occasion, Su and I were invited to a function hosted by Prince Edward on the stage of the Bloomsbury Theatre in London. My Australian friend Cheryl Cartlidge, who was at the event, gave her impression of the event and in particular my reaction: "I was acting as Su's dresser in the quick change from the 'Peggy' outfit to that mad pink and metallic bubble skirt. We all met the Prince later and it was the first time I had seen anyone hit royalty. HRH said something cheeky to Su (I WISH I could remember what) and Su in her exuberance thumped him on the arm. You in turn then nearly had a fit 'cos she'd hit him - you went white and literally nearly collapsed, I think I recall your knees buckling ('course it could've been a touch of the drama queen) - and your reaction was funnier than anything else; we all fell about laughing more at that!"

Broadway - almost a 'Funny Girl'

I did not want to be known as 'Peter Pollard' so I made sure that I had my own life and became more involved in the King's Cross Boys' Club, which had its meetings every month in the school yard across from our front door. I was the chairman and in that capacity helped the team to raise funds and organise events for many needy boys in the area. Of course, there were some 'smart' people who shook their heads saying how awful it was for a gay to be involved in a boys' club - my angry response to that was to say, "My name is Peter not Peda!" which seemed to assuage their fears. I truly loved being involved and the whole board was dedicated to the club. Being fairly high profile I was able to attract a bit more publicity than usual, which seemed to help the club. The committee of which I was chairman was totally dedicated to helping the very needy boys in our area - we sometimes held meetings in our lounge which of course thrilled the board as they were served tea and coffee by the legend Su Pollard. They were business men, shop owners, teachers etc and we used to mostly have our meetings in an abandoned church hall directly opposite our home in Islington. All of a sudden we were advised that we were to be thrown out of the building as the church wished to sell a part of it. Su and I were furious and approached the *Islington Gazette* who wrote a very critical piece on the actions of the church which helped enormously.

One day I received an invitation in the mail to attend a 'thank you' supper at Buckingham Palace hosted by the Duke of Edinburgh who was the President of all the London Boys' Clubs. After a police security check I received my official invitation with car stickers but as I had no car I went by a black taxi that drove me through the Palace gates and into the courtyard and entrance through which one sees all of the heads of states and the Queen herself enter. I was led upstairs and into a stunning, large room overlooking the huge garden where the garden parties are held. Because it was a Boys' Club event the entire guest list of about 30 comprised of all men. I was determined to check every corner and, of course, I had to use the toilet, which was disguised to fit in with the wallpaper. We all chatted together for a while and had drinks and nibbles until the Duke arrived. He made a very short speech thanking us and then spent over an hour chatting to us all as a group and individually - I was nervous but not nervous enough not to enjoy the occasion. This meant more to me than I could express because it meant that I was being accepted as just me, Peter Keogh, and the honour of being asked to the Palace had nothing to do with me being married to Su Pollard. When I left England to return to Australia years later, the Boys' Club sent me the most exceptional letter that I treasure to this day.

As my life was hurling along at a crazy pace, so were my insecurities. I felt increasingly that I was becoming just an accessory of Su's. I had always suffered from the most horrific migraines - with projectile vomiting - the whole works. For some reason the migraines started to increase and several times I had to go to an Emergency Department where I was once given a pethidine shot that not only made the physical pain disappear but also the emotional pain. I decided that I had best seek some sort of psychological help urgently before I started to 'doctor shop' to obtain more pethidine shots. I found a psychologist who worked from his home near Hampstead. He thought the migraines were being caused by the stress of suppressing gay urges and decided to show me photographs of men in various stages of undress, though not remotely pornographic, and asked me to describe in detail what I felt when I looked at the photos. I then realised that he was so far off the mark in diagnosing my problem that there was no point in returning. At the same time, my old friend, Stan Suiter, from my Ampol office days in Perth, who by now was a fully trained psychiatric 'sister', arrived for a short visit with his friend from New Zealand. While he was with us, I had another major migraine. He made me go to bed and as he mopped my very wet brow in between vomiting, he talked me through areas that he felt were some of the issues behind my migraines, none of which were the same as the psychologist had suggested. That was the last migraine I had for years until I had the two heart attacks in 2012. Can you imagine how bad it is when a true hypochondriac actually has serious health issues?

Su's profile kept growing, and while the publicity was what brought her to the attention of the public and producers, what kept her there was her talent - in so many areas. I used to really push her into diversifying her career. I had seen Debbie Reynolds act many times and believed that Su had the talent to put together her own act in similar fashion to Debbie's, so we did just that and called the show *A Song... A Frock... and A Tinkle* written, produced and directed by Richard Kates.

The show played to great acclaim at the Donmar Warehouse in Covent Garden - where I met a young fan, Mike Gattrell, who I have just recently renewed acquaintance with on Facebook after all these years. Su also had another fan at that time, Rob Cope, who followed Su's career from the time he was very young and through his loyalty and support of both of us, he and his family have become a part of our families. It was marvellous when he visited Australia with his wonderful parents, Ivan and Shirl.

Friends from New York who were on the QE2 with us also owned a small but classy restaurant/club in New York called Park 10 on 10 Park Avenue and they booked Su's show for a weekend, which was very well received. They also had the rights to a revival of the musical of *Funny Girl* - the story of Fanny Brice, which was Barbra Streisand's stepping stone to superstardom. They wanted to open the show in London and, if successful, transfer to Broadway and they wanted Su to star in it. I, of course, enthusiastically suggested that Su would be mad not to consider the offer, but she had reservations for various reasons. Not one to give up, I persuaded her to have an extended meeting with all parties involved before she made her final decision. She finally agreed to have the meeting. The only condition required to produce the show was that the songwriter, Jule Styne, who wrote the score of *Funny Girl*, had final approval of the person cast in the lead role. Su was flown to New York to have a private meeting/audition with Jule Styne in his apartment. I was not there but was told that after Su had sung and read for Jule, he was happy to give the show the go ahead. Much excitement ensued, but not long after Su returned to London, she decided against taking it after seeking the opinions of several people close to her including her dad, agent and others. Her reasons elude me to this day because I think that she was born to play the role. We didn't see much of the Park 10 chaps after that - sadly!

I really think it a shame that Su's talents as a dramatic actress have not been realised - apart from a season at the Open Air Theatre in Regent's Park as the nurse in *Romeo and Juliet*. She was the performer who most touched hearts in *Hi-de-Hi!* and her range of talents is formidable. Hopefully, she will be offered a more challenging role soon.

While in New York, Su and I did the entire tourist thing except for one thing - Su running into Sardi's Restaurant on Broadway and yelling - 'Salmonella!' We were also invited to a cocktail party which was for me more of a highlight than it was for Su because I was an enormous fan of the Golden Years of MGM musicals and at the party there were several of the stars from that era. One of them was the petite and still cute Jane Powell, who had naturally grey hair but still looked almost the same as she did in *Seven Brides for Seven Brothers*. We discussed at length her experiences touring her show to Sydney a few years earlier. We also met the very tall and very glamorous Alexis Smith, who was with her husband Craig Stevens of Peter Gunn fame. Then there was the matinee idol Van Johnson who had aged - a lot. He was also deaf as a post and had a hearing aid in both ears. He appeared to be a bit dithery and also quite gay - but very affable! To my horror, Su went up to him and told him that her mum loved him and then said, "Are you married or gay chuck?"

To which he replied, "Well I'm not married dear!"

Whilst in America we caught up with some old friends for a week in Palm Springs, Vince Fronza and Ken Fosler, who were Liberace's neighbours and best friends. Liberace had passed away under very sad and public circumstances only a matter of weeks prior to our arrival and Vince and Ken took us on a private tour of Liberace's home. We were stunned at the grandeur of his home - everything you may have heard about his home was true - even his own private chapel. We both found the tour extremely sad and Ken and Vince were still in mourning at the loss of their dear friend. Recently seeing the movie *Behind the Candelabra* brought back quite a few memories of the splendour of the place.

Back in London Su was headlining with other big stars at a television spectacular being taped at The London Hippodrome. One of the other stars was Dusty Springfield, who was magnificent in the show, but I believe was creating major dramas behind the scenes. However, all was forgiven once she opened her mouth to sing. We had all heard about Dusty being a bit of a diva but Su said she spent a lot of time with her one-on-one during rehearsals and she felt Dusty was full of sadness more than anything. She put up so many barriers it was hard to get too close to her. Dusty's voice, however, was unbelievable and Su came away from the experience more of a fan than ever.

Su was also a guest on the big London Telethon with Cilla Black as a fellow guest. During the final number I noticed that Ms Black cleverly maneuvered herself closer and closer to the cameras, so that all of the other guests looked like they were her backing singers. I wasn't impressed. At about the same time, Su was awarded the Rear of the Year and that 'honour' made news from London to Sydney!

This is 'Our' Life

In 1987, we went back to Perth for a big family Christmas. Whilst there we spent some time on the idyllic Rottnest Island - 12 miles off the coast, just one hour's boat trip from Fremantle but a thousand miles from cares. My sister, Patsy, and her husband, Carey, managed the general store on the island and they had a cute cottage a few yards from the water's edge where the whole family gathered and Su was a very welcome guest. She was as one of the family and joined in all of the activities with gusto - and no one 'gustos' more than Su. We received a call from the BBC asking us if we could please go to the Fremantle Yacht Club on New Year's Eve, where the America's Cup was won, and do a live hook-up to say 'Happy New Year' to London with Dennis Waterman and Rula Lenska, who had just got married in Perth. It was a glorious night and we did the link as the sun set and then had a bit of a party with the commodore of the yacht club and Rula and Dennis. She looked exquisite and Dennis was a hoot - they were both very happy at that time.

In 1989, I received a phone call from the researchers at *This is Your Life*, which was hosted by Michael Aspel. They asked my help in organising Su's *TIYL*. They stressed that it had to be strictly secret and that if Su suspected anything at any time they would cancel the whole episode. Keeping anything secret from Su is never easy - she loves a gossip as do I and I had to be so careful not to let anything slip. There were so many phone calls at odd hours that Su at one time said she thought I was having an affair! The plan was to do the 'hit' - turn up and surprise her with the big red book - on stage during the curtain calls of the pantomime *Dick Whittington* at the Richmond Theatre in which she was starring. Her favourite line in the play was, of course, 'Twenty miles and still no sign of Dick!'

After several months of preparation, which included flying my sister Patsy, husband, Carey, and their baby, Brodie, to London as a surprise, the date and time were fixed. At the time, Su's parents, Hilda and Don, were staying with my parents in Perth so they flew them back to London but filmed them sending greetings while they were standing in front of a backdrop of Perth giving the impression they were still there. But of course, at the very end of the show they were to walk on stage to greet what they hoped would be a very shocked, but thrilled, Su.

With the help of my sister, who was ensconced in the Holiday Inn at Swiss Cottage, we managed to smuggle a few of Su's favourite clothes into the theatre for her to change into after the 'hit'. As Su was taking her curtain calls, onto the stage walked Michael Aspel with the red book, to the screams of the audience who saw him before Su did. When he finally gave her the book she started to punch his arm over and over - out of shock and delight - the poor man must have been black and blue the next day. The audience was invited to stay while the set was changed - and every single one of them did - joined by all of the theatre staff who stood in the aisles. It was the most hilarious taping and afterwards we had the best party in the foyers. Michael Aspel was, and is, probably the nicest person I ever met in the industry in England.

After the excitement of *TIYL* we settled back into a bit of a routine. We were still being asked to all kinds of events. On one occasion we were asked to attend Michael Jackson's concert at Wembley Stadium - in the Royal Box. However, even though we were quite close to the stage there was a big delay between what we could see and the sound we heard, which quite spoiled the event so I decided to go to the guests' bar for a drink. On the way, I passed a lady who looked as though she had already spent quite a lot of time at the bar - it looked like Elaine Page - but to be fair it was just a very brief passing and it was quite dark.

Su and I frequented many gay bars while we were married where she was treated like royalty - come to think of it I guess I was too - if you get my drift! We were often at the Black Cap in Camden and the Vauxhall Tavern where we first saw the brilliant Lily Savage. We also came to know, and really like, such great characters as Adrella, Dockyard Doris, who was such a sweet man and The Trollettes who all loved Su and she adored them. Through Su I met some of the most exceptional people, not all of whom were in show business. One couple was John Addy and Antony Porter, who initially were fans but eventually became second family. Their generosity was exceptional and they kindly asked us on numerous occasions to stay in their most beautiful - to me being a simple Aussie - 'castle' in Huddersfield. It was huge yet very much a home. Two things stand out about their 'castle' - one being the huge dragon which lived under the staircase. I'm not sure of the correct name of it but it looked like an enormous Australian goanna! It was bordering on tame and both boys looked after it lovingly, almost as if it were a pet dog. It was wonderful although I almost passed out when I first saw it. They also had turned a large mezzanine room into a mini Catholic chapel - with the priest's vestments, statues and beautiful paintings. I spent some special contemplative moments there.

For one of John Addy's birthday parties, they booked the glorious Armathwaite Hall in the Lake District, which was, in fact, unknown to us, a mystery murder night - where guests and staff were dropping like flies. The highlight of the night was Lily Savage - aka Paul O'Grady - a friend of the boys, performing. We stayed overnight with others including Beryl Reid and Barbara Windsor. During the evening Su kept whistling her famous whistle through her fingers, however, it made Beryl's blood curdle and she told Su so - it was the most stunning event. John and Antony were a very special couple. John was the human dynamo, while Antony was the more serious of the two but still great fun. Antony passed away several years ago - yet another taken too soon.

As Su was often away touring, we started to drift apart - never with animosity - it was just that distance and time apart did not help the relationship. We had an old friend from Playhouse days in Perth - Cheryl Cartlidge - who had moved to London to find work and she stayed with us for a short period until she found work at Sadler's Wells Theatre in their marketing/publicity department. One weekend while Su was touring and I had a few free days, we foolishly decided to go to Amsterdam because she had never been. We went to King's Cross Station to board the train but all of the electronic departure signs were out of order, so we were told to go to Victoria Station where another train was waiting. We arrived at Victoria and boarded the train - well, we tried to but it was full of loud, aggressive football fans. We walked into one end of the carriage and straight out the other end and decided that we had best fly so we headed to Heathrow. Troubles there too - engine problems so our gate number was changed - but finally we caught our flight. All the way to Amsterdam I was a wreck because I felt that all the mishaps were some kind of a message from 'above' and that the plane would crash with headlines saying *'Hi-de-Hi!* star's husband killed in plane crash while on tryst with unknown woman'. We finally arrived safely and checked into a little flat on a canal and went out to a Dutch dinner at a nice little restaurant and afterwards headed for one of the coffee shops with the hash brownies. We had some coffee and cake and bought some hash laced chocolates to take back to the apartment. Cheryl went to her bed while I decided to go to the Amstel Tavern where Su and I had, on a previous visit, had the best time. I showered and made my way to the Amstel but I was back in the flat after just 15 minutes. The club was closed for the first time. A sign on the door explained that the owner's father had died. Talk about an omen - we should obviously never have gone to Amsterdam.

Sacha, Separation, Death and Divorce

Looking back on my experiences, it reads like a charmed life, and in many ways it was. However, I have to say that for a lot of that time I felt totally alone. I still had no confidence and each time Su and I attended a function I was wet through with stress. I used to perspire so much that at one time I used to pin sanitary napkins into the arm of my suits to catch the sweat! I used to always think that people were only being friendly to me because I was married to such a big star - and often they were and that really hurt. However, now, exactly 30 years later, many of those people are my dearest friends but at the time I was never sure of anyone's motives.

Su and I decided that it might be a good idea to have a trial separation. There was no animosity, there never has been, but we weren't as happy as we once were. I went back to see my sister and her family in Melbourne. At that time my ex, John Frost was producing the musical, *Big River* at Her Majesty's Theatre and he asked me along to see the show. I adored it. Afterwards, I was in John's office when there was a knock on the door and in walked this person who I vaguely recognised - the gap in the teeth! He was introduced as Sacha Mahboub, the wardrobe master. Being my usual tactful self I said, "Have I had you?" whereupon he stormed out of the office and a few minutes later he called John and told him that once that rude person - me - had left the office he would come back. John was a bit shocked and suggested that I apologise so the following day I sent him a note that said 'I'm so sorry - by the way my phone number is... oops!' There was no response for days and then he called and agreed to meet me in the foyer of the theatre after a performance for a drink. He turned up with some chap hanging off his arm with whom he'd been having a 'thing' but deigned to spend five minutes with me. All just camp fun but neither of us was remotely interested in anything other than being pals. John Frost was the perfect host during my stay in Melbourne. Knowing I was really feeling pretty miserable and very confused he made sure I tagged along to all the cast events and there were many.

A few nights after Sach and I met, John asked me to another cast party, which the whole company attended, including Sach and a chap who was actively pursuing me. All night Sach barely spoke to me because he totally refused to be involved with a married man, which I understood and respected. I was staying with my now estranged sister and her family, which was really nice because they were very supportive in this confusing moment in my life. I found that by taking their kids, one of whom is my Godchild - Nathan, to various shows I was able to put my feelings on the back burner for a time. To be honest I was starting to relax and enjoy the company of the group and was honestly stunned that there were guys that fancied me, which confused me even more. One of the crew came up to me at the bar after a performance one night and we had a long chat - nothing more - and the next night he presented me with a beautiful envelope and inside was a long and very moving poem, which I still have, about his feelings for me. Years ago I would have jumped straight into his bed because it was the only way I knew to express my gratitude, but this time I was very flattered but also able to tell him that I was in the middle of a very sad separation and not remotely able to return his feelings. A first for me!

In the meantime, I had some quality time with my family and also had a few more meetings with Sach - all platonic, mainly because we just had so many mutual friends. We became quite close and when I decided to return to London to sort out the situation with Su, Sach agreed to come along and catch up with some friends working in shows in London. Su was very sweet to Sach, inviting him to functions and also tapings of her new show, *You Rang M'lord*. Around this time I was asked to house-sit for Gloria Hunniford for four days in her beautiful home in

Sevenoaks, Kent, which could have been more correctly named The Oak because during an infamous storm six of the oaks were damaged or destroyed. Those four days gave me some breathing space to think through my current situation with Su. We then decided to give it another try, but she had to immediately go on tour. A few days later in the middle of the night I received a distressing call from my younger sister, Patsy, advising me that my father had just died. She was naturally hysterical and I was in shock - so many emotions running through me. I called Su who told me to get on to the first plane home to Mum and the family! Sach stayed in London to look after our house and our two cats, Dulcie and Michael, named after the actors Michael Denison and Dulcie Gray of course!

For the entire flight home I was finding it hard to comprehend that Dad was no longer with us. I also felt such guilt about all of the issues I had put Dad through over the years and now I was even thinking about separating from Su, which would have upset him terribly. Being a Catholic I also felt that Dad knew and saw everything that I was doing and thinking, even in death. I was met at Perth airport by my sister and her husband and taken back to my parents' home where this time there was only Mum. All of us were very much in shock but Mum appeared to be quite strong, organising the awful matter of deciding what suit to bury Dad in etc. However her true feelings surfaced when she told us that she would attend Dad's Requiem Mass but there was no way she could go to his grave site. She mourned privately and deeply. A few days after I arrived home, I became very ill - uncontrollable vomiting and diarrhoea that caused my heart once again to go into atrial fibrillation. It was probably the beginning of my current heart issues. My doctor, who is now a close friend, was at a loss to know what the cause of my illness was. I was able to recover sufficiently to attend Dad's funeral, which was heartbreakingly sad. I just kept looking at the coffin finding it beyond comprehension that my Dad was lying in there - dead! So many things unsaid - so many issues unresolved! I would then, and still do, talk to him through occasional prayers.

After Dad's funeral we all felt that Mum needed some support so I decided to stay with her in Perth for a time and that time was extended regularly. The longer I stayed in Australia, the less I wanted to go back to England... and the marriage. I renewed so many old friendships and it was wonderful being able to be close to family and especially Mum as she adapted to life without Dad. Su and I spoke regularly and eventually both agreed we should get a divorce. Later, Sach came back to Australia and we became very close. I have to say that I think one of the reasons we have lasted so long in our relationship, 23 years, is because for a long time we were just friends and gradually we came to care about each other more deeply. When all this was happening, word leaked out somehow to the press and suddenly there were articles saying that I had run off with a 'nude dancer'. Well he wasn't nude when we ran off and, in fact, only once in his life did he dance even close to nude, semi-nude, at a television channel's New Year's Eve party in Australia many years before we ever met. Mum then started to receive calls from the press in London asking if she knew where I was; was I divorcing Su and was I living with the 'nude dancer'? She lied, of course, and told them that she had no idea. I was actually sitting in her kitchen at the time. One day there was a knock on her front door and when she answered it there were two people, one with a camera, from the *News of the World*. After she told them to leave, they stayed parked outside the house. To leave, I had to get into the car boot and be driven to wherever I was going. Finally, it became ridiculous so I decided to give them a story if they would then leave us alone. They agreed and I gave them the interview. I tried to keep it as light and humorous as possible.

KNOW HOW TO MAKE LOVE TO MY SU

● Hi-de-Hi gay hubby tells all

Peter had to stand trial on a fraud charge.

"I was innocent and I was cleared, but it was a dreadful time that even now I still have nightmares about," he says.

His previous sex life came out at the trial. And at the school where he was teaching some parents staged a demonstration over their children being taught by a homosexual.

He recalls: "Everyone was wonderful and refused to let me resign.

"But we got a lot of hate mail and it reached the point when we would lie in bed sick with fear.

"A message on the answerphone was the worst. A cold, hard voice told Su that there was a contract out on both our lives. We told the police and they took it extremely seriously."

Both narrowly avoided serious injury when a large lump of concrete was hurled at them as they sat drinking together in a bar.

"It just missed us," Peter says. "We could have easily been killed.

"Once a guy stood out...

former gay lovers confronted Su when they were out together. Peter reveals: "He came straight up and told her, 'I've had your husband!'

"But Su was marvellous. She just turned to him and asked, 'Was he any good, darling?'

"The bloke was tall, dark and very good looking. I'd enjoyed a one-night stand with him a year or so before.

"He was furious when he saw me with Su and probably hoped to cause a scene. But when all Su did was laugh he flounced off in a huff.

"The thing was that she was genuinely interested in whether he'd thought I was any good in bed. She wanted to know all about him, all the gory details. She was fascinated by all the men in my life.

"Su was always so understanding. When another ex-lover of mine came to see us she couldn't have been nicer to him."

Peter admits that he still felt attracted to men after their marriage. "But not enough to be un...

After much soul searching and many tears, Su and I decided to proceed with the divorce. It was a very sad time for both of us. There were a number of articles appearing with all kinds of theories as to why we were divorcing but only we knew how simple the reasons were, so we didn't respond to any of the stories and quietly went our separate ways. Quite apart from the sorrow of us breaking up I was also incredibly sad to leave England. During my life with Su I was lucky enough to see much more of the country than I ever dreamed I would, including a scary helicopter flight from Cornwall to Scotland where Su was opening some kind of function. The pilot asked us both to keep our eyes open for power lines, which totally freaked us out. The beauty of the country astounded me. I was so used to a country where there was very little sign of seasons changing, whereas in England the changes were huge and every season had its own unique beauty. As I write this I think of all of the reasons why I loved living in England. First and foremost are the people; their overwhelming hospitality, sense of humour, wonderful manners and the way they accepted and embraced me in so many ways, especially during some very bad times. I've made incredible friends and I learned so much about myself. It's where I learned to love deeply, a place where I lost a part of myself, but above all, a place where I could be free to live, for the first time in my life. My years in England were the most exciting, sad, funny, rewarding and fulfilling of my life to date. I still miss the buzz on Shaftsbury Avenue, the tube, the pubs - gay and straight - my first white Christmas, all of the theatres Su played in all over the country and much more. I may be many thousands of miles away now but every memory and every friend stays with me wherever I go and will forever.

Sacha is three years older than me and when we met, the last thing we wanted or needed was a relationship. I was thinking about separating from Su and he had been in and out of a few relationships, so flying solo again was a very attractive prospect. He was very volatile when we met and probably more so afterwards. It has been said that living with me can be hard work - hard to believe, I know! In fact, the most common comment I hear still is people saying to Sach, "How on earth do you cope with Peter - you poor thing?" Sach had a very sad upbringing. He was raised in an orphanage in Queensland where he suffered the worst kind of abuse, physical and mental. A few years ago the government opened a big enquiry into the abuse at the orphanage and Sach's case was one of those used as an example of the severity of the cruelty and he finally received an official apology and a token payment. The apology was what meant the world to Sach - the recognition of the horrors he had suffered because sometimes he felt as if he was totally alone. He has found it hard to talk about and often when he did talk about it, he felt as though no one believed him. One of the incidents that I found incredibly cruel was one Christmas he received a fairly large box which he opened only to find another smaller one and then another - finally in the last one was a note saying, 'This is all you deserve from Santa this year!'

Sach went on to work as a 'jackaroo', an Australian term for a cowboy, for a while. It is a terribly butch job, droving cattle and shearing, plus fixing fences. It would have killed me in a week. However, his dream was to be a dancer and he never gave up on his dream. Eventually he was in the chorus of some of the biggest musicals in the country and then he put together and starred in a cabaret show that he took to Europe!

Life after Su - Health Scares

After the furore had died down, I thought that the best tonic for us all, especially Mum, was to leave the country. Sacha, Mum and I went to America for a couple of months. Starting in Hawaii, Mum's favourite, moving on to Los Angeles where we grabbed our bags and rushed straight from the airport to the Pantages Theatre to catch the last performance of Debbie Reynolds in the stage version of her hit movie *The Unsinkable Molly Brown,* leaving our cases in the box office. We also obtained tickets to a taping of the television series *The Golden Girls*, which was great fun.

We then drove to Las Vegas where Mum's favourite memory is a drag show at the Riviera Hotel. We also naturally visited the Debbie Reynolds Hotel and Casino but Debbie was on tour so we were photographed all over her hotel, even standing in her private car bay in front of the sign saying, 'RESERVED FOR DEBBIE REYNOLDS'. We also met and had a brief chat with Debbie's son Todd Fisher.

Then we went on to Orlando and Disney World. We did everything on a budget and stayed for a month at a Day's Inn near Disney Village for $39 a night - all in one room. But it was the most special time. We laughed ourselves to sleep every night, toured such beautiful places as St Augustine, the oldest city in America where we stayed in a guest house very much like Tara in *Gone With the Wind* and even drank from Ponce de Leon's Fountain of Youth - to no avail I hasten to add. The streets were preserved in the period, 1565, and transport through the town was by horse and buggy.

In New York we stayed in a hotel on Broadway, saw a couple of shows and had breakfast at the Windows on the World restaurant on the 106th floor of the now destroyed Twin Towers. We couldn't believe how high it was and, on the day that we were there, we were well above the clouds and could only see little bits of the street below as the clouds shifted. The thought of a person jumping from there turns my blood cold. Mum was having such a wonderful time travelling, it was heartwarming. We browsed through Tiffany's, shopped at Macy's, went to mass and lit a candle for Dad at St Patrick's Cathedral and enjoyed being a family.

Our last day in New York was Christmas Day and it started to snow, which delighted Mum. She loved watching the steam coming up from the streets, just like in the movies she had seen. Our next stop was Toronto so we headed to La Guardia Airport and as we were waiting at the gate having coffee, a tiny plane with two propellers, that looked like something Howard Hughes might have built, pulled up and started to unload passengers onto the tarmac - it was too low for the sky bridge. I freaked out and rushed to the airlines desk and asked where that plane was flying to and they told me - Toronto! Mum and Sach both said I turned whiter than white - to their great amusement. We finally boarded and there were two seats each side of one aisle. It held about 30 passengers and the only concession to it being Christmas Day was a tiny piece of tinsel wrapped around the Exit sign. Sach and Mum sat alongside each other and I sat behind Sach holding his hand which he held over his head as we rattled down the runway. The noise was deafening, we could barely hear each other even if we yelled and, believe me, I was yelling! Because the plane was so small it was not pressurised and as a result could only fly at a certain altitude and speed, which didn't appear to be very high or very fast. In fact, at one stage I recall looking out of the window and I swear that cars were going faster than we were! After finally landing we caught a bus to the Royal York Hotel where they gave us the Royal Suite on the top floor - I have no idea why, just lucky I guess. It was very grand. It snowed all night and the next day we hired a car and drove to Niagara Falls. Words cannot describe the grandeur of the Falls - and the noise. After few hours we drove to Niagara-on-the-Lake, which is a small town in Southern Ontario where the Niagara River meets Lake Ontario. It turned out to be one of our favourite towns in Canada - old world charm and service. We had lunch at the Prince of Wales Hotel and it was like being in a time warp where everything was exactly as it was 100 years ago, including some of the staff! After lunch we built a snowman outside the hotel, which delighted Mum, who seemed to gain confidence each day and the sadness of Dad's sudden passing seemed to dim a little. She enjoyed every minute of every day of the trip and her enthusiasm was infectious.

When we got back to Australia, Sach and I both needed to be employed so we found jobs at a large ticketing agency, BOCS Ticketing. We hated it initially and after a week we went on a lunch break and decided we wouldn't go back. We had no skills with a computer or typing and every aspect of the job involved a computer. We told our boss, Terryl Moir, that we were out of there but she told us in no uncertain terms that we would be staying. She sat with us for a couple of days, one on one, and trained us and her patience and kindness were the main reasons we decided stay - me for 19 years. I detected an edge from some members of the staff who were aware of my life with Su and perhaps even the trial and felt it their duty to bring me down a peg or two but we hung on and became friends with some of the most special people now in our lives.

Not long after we got back from the trip, Mum discovered a lump in her upper arm and had it removed and tested. The results came back and shockingly they indicated that she had Non-Hodgkin's Lymphoma so chemo and radiation therapy were started immediately. The whole family gathered to help Mum through this dreadful time. Every morning she would wake up with big clumps of hair on her pillow, so Sach shaved her head and as he finished he planted a huge kiss on her bald head - causing us all to fill up. My sister, Patsy, and her husband, Carey, and Sach were her main carers, as she bravely battled the awful disease. I was at work most days and tried to be there for her whenever I could, but Sach, only working casually, had more time to spend with Mum and they became extremely close. After about a year of debilitating treatment, it seemed that Mum's cancer was in remission and we cautiously celebrated.

Things were calm for a time - me finally adapting to a quieter life after the whirl of England and Su. Being a hypochondriac I needed to find a compassionate doctor who would tolerate me and my illnesses - real and imagined. I was lucky to find two - Dr Paul Cook and his soon-to-be wife Dr Farah Ahmed. Paul was Mum's doctor at the time, and she adored him. Paul was the best of doctors but also a nice and good man with a wicked sense of humour. One particular memory was, after yet another battery of tests for everything and anything; he called me into the surgery. He sat me down and told me that he had some good news and some bad news. He said, "The good news is that you have AIDS." I felt myself start to shake, bottom lip quivering and I thought *If that's the good news what the hell is the bad news?* He then said, "The bad news is that you're still gay!" Of course I did not have AIDS and I was actually able to laugh after I had hit him a few times. In spite, or maybe because of that day, we remain the very best of friends. We attended his wedding to the beautiful Farah and they attend all of our important occasions. They have both been there for us throughout the series of illnesses in our family and have given us all invaluable and loving support. They are not only exceptional and dedicated doctors but also the most compassionate and good human beings and we are blessed to have them in our lives. They have to be saints for handling my galloping hypochondria.

Life rolled along at a leisurely pace. We acquired three cats and four dogs and the most special and dear friends and then, just as things seemed to be near perfect, another hiccup tuned our lives upside down. Sach had been feeling more tired than usual and also finding it difficult to urinate so off he went to see Dr Paul, who referred him to a specialist. Tests were done and Mum and I were sitting in our local pub having a drink while Sach went to pick up his test results. My mobile rang and it was Sach, who sounded in shock and he indeed was. He had just been told that he had a particularly aggressive form of prostate cancer and an operation was needed immediately to remove the whole prostate, a transurethral resection of the prostate, to hopefully save his life. Sach had not spent even a day in hospital before this and he was mortified. Now it was the family's turn to give Sach the same support as he had given Mum. It was so hard leaving him in hospital the morning of his operation, after being told of all of the risks involved. He was also warned that he may need a permanent catheter and may also be impotent for the rest of his life.

The operation was long and dangerous. They apparently took a lot of his stomach out temporarily and rested it on his side and he was cut from his navel to his pubic region. I came to see him that night and he looked terrible. It was a bigger shock because I had not seen him with anything more than a cold previously. There were tubes and drips from and into every orifice. As soon as I saw him I started to feel faint so I told him to move over for me to lie down - he just smiled! The following day I went to see him and he was a bit cheerier and taking calls from celebrities he had worked with all over the world, always saying as loud as he could, "Hellooooooo so-and-so," so the staff could hear that he knew famous people - so funny! He also had a raised section of bed over his lower half. When I asked him why, he pulled back his bed covers and his testicles looked like two black, blue and purple bowling balls. Two gay friends brought him three tiny camp pillows to rest his testicles on while they healed. A month after the operation, he saw the specialist about the two side effects mentioned above as a possible consequence of the operation - all I'll say is that only one of them eventuated. The whole exercise made me appreciate how precious life is and also how easily we take our partners for granted. I tried to be a better partner after Sach's cancer scare and I think I succeeded - for a couple of weeks.

Not to be outdone, it was then my turn. I had been having chest pains that we all thought might possibly be heart related but turned out be caused by gallstones and they needed to remove was marked. He found Topol to be obnoxious, big-headed and very rude and totally charmless. As the saying goes, 'he must have had a heart of gold because the rest of him was flint'. To add insult to injury, Sach's hotel in Wellington was evacuated in the middle of the night when a raging storm set off fire alarms. He called me from the street - drenched to his skin dressed only in his undies and counting the hours until the tour was finished.

On his return to Perth he was asked to do the same for his hero Mikhail Barisknykov at His Majesty's Theatre. Unfortunately it was a case of one's heroes not living up to expectations. Mikhail was certainly pleasant enough but very much involved in Mikhail. One night during curtain calls, Mikhail could not be found because he was in the Green Room watching himself on television in the movie *White Knights*. However, he was kind enough to sign a T-shirt for Sach, which he has framed in our lounge room.

Then suddenly health issues developed for me and, unfortunately, they were not imagined! Late one night we had taken Mum to Emergency because she was going through quite a bad time with her chemo. As we were leaving the hospital I said to Mum and Sach that I was surprised at the amount of lightning in the sky on such a clear night but they said there wasn't one flash of lightning - so we went straight back to Emergency and they diagnosed a detached retina. I had to go to bed and not move my head all night and the next morning it was lasered. It wasn't too bad really but a few weeks later my eyes were tested and I was almost bloody blind and I was told that I needed a corneal graft. A few years earlier Mum had a similar operation where they put an anaesthetic needle straight into her eyeball while she was awake. I told my surgeon that if that was what was in store for me I would rather train my Maltese poodle to be a guide dog! Eventually I persuaded him to knock me out in a chair in the waiting room and they then wheeled me into theatre and did the procedure. The worst thing was that I could feel the stitches under my eye lid but it improved my vision dramatically.

So far so good, then a couple of months later I was running across the road outside work and tripped - again, but this time broke my rib. Not a good thing to happen to a person terrified of dying of a heart attack. Every time I laughed or coughed or sneezed I nearly passed out from the pain, which I was never sure wasn't from a heart attack. I used to go to bed with one hand resting on the phone so I could dial 000 instantly if needed.

We both kept working at BOCS Ticketing with Sach doing the odd theatre job as well. One of them was working with Patricia Routledge in *The Importance of Being Earnest*. She was vaguely friendly but gave instruction that she would not sign or discuss anything to do with *Keeping up Appearances*. We both also worked on an ill-fated production of *Peter Pan* in the wardrobe department. Sach looked after Christopher Cazenove who used to gargle with Listerine before each show and then drink it, while I looked after a person of 'diminished stature' who spent the whole show in a dog suit! One of my duties was to wait in the wings for him to come bounding off stage where I had to rip his dog head off and spray his face with water. However, at the first dress rehearsal I was in a panic and in the dark I accidentally sprayed his face and mouth with hair spray - not a happy puppy! On the opening night of *Peter Pan* they had a set with a backdrop of the roofs of London. I was on one side of the stage, bored witless, and I suddenly saw Sach on the other side, so I just waved at him and proceeded to walk across the stage to chat with him. What I didn't know was the audience could see me and to them it looked like I was walking across the London skyline, a bit like Mary Poppins, boy was I in trouble - again - still! This production also had major management issues and closed in its first week.

Meanwhile at The Maj - His Majesty's Theatre - where I was box office manager, we were very excited because we had Maggie Smith arriving in *Talking Heads*. We were given strict instructions not to stay in her line of vision, only speak if spoken too and never ever mention anything to do with *Harry Potter*. The stage door person was told to tell people who left any *Harry Potter* memorabilia to be signed that they were wasting their time. However, when she arrived the exact opposite happened. She was extremely sweet, always smiled and spoke if we passed in a corridor and even had short chats. In fact she was a total charmer.

Monday to Friday. However, when she arrived she saw our little Daiwoo Matiz and told us that she was perfectly happy for us to use that for her transport and as for the other rider conditions, well, she was in Perth for almost the month and worked seven days a week and often until very late at night never once complaining and then we would go back to her hotel for notes and drinks in the al fresco cafe. Perth's wonderful Lord Mayor, Lisa Scaffidi, kindly asked Debbie to lunch at Council House to welcome her to Perth. Debbie loved Lisa and was having the best time but once again the director was the fly in the ointment and insisted Debbie could only have an hour off for the lunch. Being a team member Debbie sadly agreed.

Long before the show was signed and sealed, we were approached by a person we thought of as a friend to do the marketing. We told her that if she felt she couldn't obtain contra deals, we still had time to cancel the show. She assured us that she could and that we should proceed. As the opening night approached we found out that no such deals existed except a contra deal for Debbie's fare with Qantas. She then offered, along with a friend of hers, to give us a loan so that the show could go on. We had no choice but to accept the loan with the most horrifying amount of interest. We were later told that this person was well-known as a bit of a snake oil salesman! In the end, the show was a huge success - everyone was paid - with friends like our publicist Lynne Burford and others charging their bare minimum fee. The sad thing was that my friend and Mum got their money back but with no profit. The people who loaned us the money were also paid back in full, though we couldn't pay the horrifying interest. They started to get heavy so we spoke to our great accountant who recommended we file for bankruptcy, which with broken hearts and shattered pride, we did!

We have no regrets because we made a huge dream come true and presented a show that people are still talking about today. Debbie Reynolds - the girl I first saw in 1952 on the silver screen, in 2012 is one of my dearest friends. Never give up on dreams. With hard work they can come true!

Commitment - Heart Attacks - Bye-de-Bye

While Debbie and Jenny were here, Sach and I decided to have a Ceremony of Commitment. John Frost flew over to be our Best Man and Debbie was our Matron-of-Honour. We had a matinee on Australia Day but no evening performance so that was the day of our Commitment Ceremony!

Certificate of Commitment

I, Jay Riordon Walsh

hereby certify that I have, on this day, according to a personally composed cultural ceremony, at

235a Forrest Street, Palmyra, Western Australia

duly solemnised a permanent relationship with the beliefs and wishes of the two persons named below, that is between

Peter Keogh
and
Sacha Mahboub

Dated this 26th day of January 2008

We were honoured to have Jay Walsh, an old and dear friend who has supported me through many stages of my life, as our celebrant. He gave us a beautiful ceremony with words he chose that touched us deeply. We had a wonderful a cappella group called Quintessence - thanks to Cheryl Cartlidge who sang, amongst others, Debbie's theme song 'Tammy', which delighted her. Debbie added that she would have happily have sung it for us herself. Being surrounded by family and friends made us feel very blessed indeed. We had the most wonderful evening - Debbie had us in stitches all night, with her PA and my best pal Jenny ending up doing the splits with my sister Patsy. A night the memories of which we will always treasure.

After another sad farewell to Debbie and Jenny we returned to work at BOCS Ticketing and basically our lives returned to normal - how I hate that word - as normal as our lives could ever be!

My next milestone was turning 65 - which I was sort of looking forward to, being able to acquire some of the benefits of being a pensioner, not that many mind you - so we had a Peter's Pensioner Party with a cake designed to look like a Pensioner's Concession

Card. We also had Paul Peacock, the star of *Irene* perform a wonderful cabaret style show for us. He first performed, in drag, as his alter ego, Sebastian Crinkle, then after dinner, as himself, he sang a selection from Broadway shows. He won every heart, including mine! He and his lovely wife have since welcomed a beautiful son into the world.

I felt that at 65 it would be wise to have a general check-up from head to toe. It was decided that I should have an echocardiogram to play it safe because Dad had died after three heart attacks. I was told to lie on my left side with my right arm over my head as the technician squirted a cold gel on the surface of a wand and swiped it all over my chest and around my heart all the time looking at the ultrasound images on a big screen near my head. Every once in a while he would turn up the volume and I could hear the loud sound of my heart beating. What I didn't understand, and what the technician was forbidden to discuss with me, was the whooshing sound after each heartbeat, which was my aortic valve regurgitating because it was unable to close properly forcing blood to leak back into my heart. I was later told the condition had caused me to have a heart attack - no, not one - TWO of the bloody things! The word 'shocked' nowhere near describes my emotions - total fear! I was told to bring my cholesterol levels down urgently, which I now have and am on daily medication.

As a way of saying a fun 'thank you' to Sach for always being there, I decided to give him a surprise 70th birthday at the Dolphin Theatre at the University of Western Australia. Madeline Joll, Kevin Hamersley, Robyn Wilson and John Doyle were generous to a fault in helping us organise the party. My sister, Patsy, and her husband, Carey, also worked hard to make it a fun night. Our old pals from Edwards Restaurant days, Alan and Marion, and Stephen and Annie, looked after the catering with their usual generosity and humour. Sach was working on the opera and (prearranged with his boss at the Opera Company) I called him and said that I had a fall at work and needed him to take me to the hospital. After a bit of a whinge he said he was on his way. He walked into the theatre where I was sitting in the stalls doing a floor show as though I was in pain. As soon as he saw me he said, "Is there no end to you?" As soon as he spoke the house curtain opened to reveal over 50 friends on the stage singing HAPPY BIRTHDAY! It was the most special night. Debbie Reynolds and Jenny and her musicians Joey and Gerry sent a video message as did Lord Mayor Lisa Scaffidi, Tina Bursill, John Frost and others.

My best friend from London days, Paul Callaghan, was our perfect MC. Every single guest was special to us all but especially to Sach. Our MD from *Irene*, Tim Cunniffe and his beautiful wife Sherry, with Paul Peacock and the multi-talented Analisa Bell, performed a medley of songs from the shows we had produced before a piece especially written by Tim that was clever, funny and very touching. I know Sach felt much loved on his 70th - he still does, and is, today!

Theatre continues to pulse through my veins. I was asked to work at Mandurah Performing Arts Centre as box office supervisor of a great team. However, I'm not sure they were quite ready for me. I have a lot of experience that I'm happy to share if it helps, but I'm very vulgar and I don't suffer fools at all. I think I've been around long enough not to worry too much about what people think as long as I'm not intentionally hurting anyone. However, I found a 40 hour week a little tiring and was not able to spend any kind of quality time with Sacha, my family, especially my mum, and friends so I decided to work two days a week - finish this memoir and enjoy every remaining second with Sacha, family my pets and finally enjoy being me - mind you - not sure 'who' or 'what' me is!

There would be no memoir, or in fact no 'me', without my mum - she's one in ten million. She turns 90 this year and never stops giving. There's also my sister, Patsy, who is generous like Mum and also funny, and her patient and tolerant husband, Carey, who has become the brother I never had but always wanted, plus their exceptional kids, Brodie and Bradley. They have been passengers on my journey and have never jumped ship for which I am forever grateful.

My sister, Patsy, and her husband Carey.

I turned 69 this year and Sach and I now live happily in Mandurah, which is about a 45 minute drive south of Perth, with our four dogs, Rudy, Bijou, Bam Bam and Mustapha. John Frost kindly invites us to all of the first nights of his productions all over Australia, which one of us usually tries to attend. Apart from being an exciting event we are also able to catch up with many of the friends we have made in the industry over the years. We often have friends stay with us for a weekend, which is always fun, and we also stay in touch with Debbie and Jenny and our friends in America and England - mostly through emails and Facebook and occasionally in person. Mum, Patsy and Carey live just a couple of miles away and we see them most weekends. Our lives are both busy and full of people we love.

My dear Mum in her 90th year - still laughing every day

Looking back at my life now, I think that of all the lessons I've learned that I would pass on if ever asked would be ironically from Shakespeare, 'To thine own self be true'. If you are not true to yourself then how can one be true to anybody else? It's often easier said than done, but believe me it is worthwhile. To be honest, I am a little envious of the freedom young gays have now compared to my youth, when we had to hide the fact from family, friends and especially employers. However, I still see many young gays all over the world being bullied - especially through social media - and feeling the only way out is suicide. I am expecting quite a bit of flack myself when some of my tales see the light of day, even now, in 2013. It is so important that those who feel the need for help know that they are NOT alone and that it is available. I have also learnt that you can never give up even when there seems absolutely no light at the end of the tunnel, as I felt during my trial in London. Once again friends saved the day, they stuck by me. I still hear in my head Jill Perryman's advice - 'right is might'. It helped me enormously through that dreadful time and it does today. Stick to the truth no matter how hard - and sometimes it can be very hard. And finally, never be afraid to dream, nor let others try and shatter your dreams. Dreams can and do come true, often in the most surprising ways.

I have lived, loved, laughed and cried a lot and have been lucky enough to have been loved a lot. I have also been blessed with the most exceptional family and friends, who have stuck by me through thick and thin, good and bad and there has been a lot of each. I think that I'm finally accepting that I am a worthwhile person and may have possibly given something of value to my friends and family. I also recognise that I am able to make people laugh without actually trying. I just wish that I had been able to do so years ago when I didn't even have the confidence to walk down the aisle of a bus. This ability to make people laugh has saved my skin so many times - especially with Sach. To Sach's great chagrin I am a terrible at nights - I find it very hard to sleep and usually end up at all hours doing all kinds of things - in fact he calls me 'Mrs. Danvers'.

As I head toward my 70th birthday, I live very much one day at a time. I have been to quite a lot of funerals of friends and family who are younger than me and also seen many of those diagnosed with dementia and Alzheimer's - the 'long goodbye', that is often much sadder than their actual death. It would have been nice to have been in a position not to have to work at our ages, but fate decreed that was not to be and to be quite frank if I have too many free days I quickly become bored and I miss the challenge of working. I'm sure it also keeps us mentally alert, it's a shame it doesn't keep the body as alert. I now look at the hands on the end of my arms and I see Dad's hands and I look at my face and I see things that do not thrill me. However I also look across the room and I see Sach. I also see our four precious dogs. I hear the phone ring and it is one of our many friends. I open my emails and there are always several from family and friends. I look at Facebook and I always get a thrill when someone clicks 'Like' under one of my comments - it's the acceptance thing again I guess. In short I have an abundance of blessings and will keep on doing whatever it is I 'do' as well as I can for as long as I can. There never seems to be a shortage of unusual experiences in my life - I truly don't know why. So I fully expect that there will be a lot more before my 'finale'! I can't wait to experience them all.

Su Pollard still works most of every year all over the world - all around England, South East Asia also Hong Kong, New Zealand and Australia. She never changes - thank goodness!

Debbie Reynolds works 40 weeks a year touring her shows. She has just finished her new book *Unsinkable* and is currently earning rave reviews for her outstanding guest performance in the new movie *Behind the Candelabra*, playing Liberace's mother. Her PA Jenny and I used email and text each other regularly until her death last month - I miss her every day.

John Frost goes from strength to strength with his productions filling theatres all over the world.

And then there's the man who saw something in me I couldn't even see myself - Sacha Mahboub was able to cut through the facade I had buried myself behind and found the 'me' I had kept hidden from the day I was born. When I see him walk into a room, it's as if a light has been turned on. We phone each other a dozen times a day - we never stop talking. I cannot imagine being in a world without him.

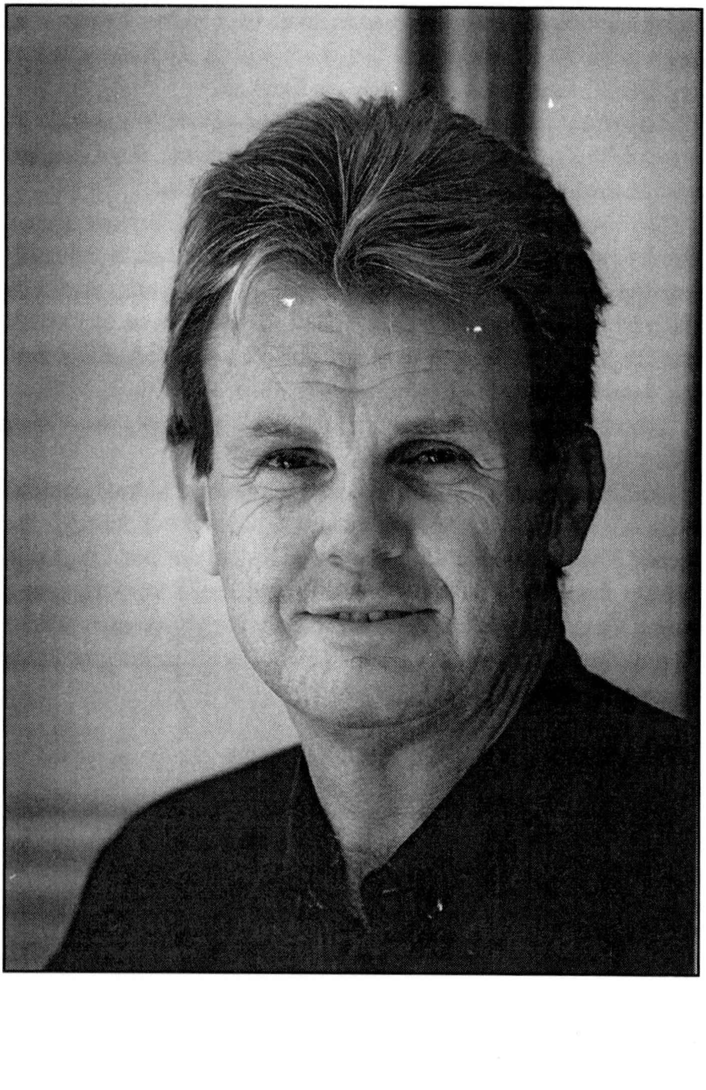

Acknowledgements

My heartfelt thanks to my family and many friends for their recollections and memories but especially Sach for his tolerance of my mood swings, day and night, as I pushed forward with this project and the delicious food regularly served at my desk. He nourished my body and spirit!

Special thanks to Editor Jan Hallam and her husband Peter for their dedication. Jan's encouragement, even when I threatened to erase every word, is appreciated. Similarly, Lynne Burford who I consider one of the top publicists in the country and who, along with David, is my dearest friend. They offered support in many ways from day one.

Debbie Reynolds' PA Jenny, who I loved dearly and who sadly passed away from cancer after a very short illness a few weeks ago, was right beside me in spirit as I typed every word.

John Frost was, well, just John Frost - brilliantly supportive in his usual cutting and hilarious fashion. I treasure his and Shane's friendship.

There are so many more special people who advised at every turn - too many to mention here but you all know who you are and I am forever grateful. Special mention to Tina Bursill and her parents, Ail and Keith, Paul Callaghan, Leanne Morton, Rob Cope, John Burbidge, Stan Suiter, Peter and Norma Powell, Cheryl and Clem, Valerie Adnams and Betty Quinlan.

Special thanks also to the people who would occasionally suggest, in a slightly sinister fashion, that I had perhaps have a rethink about writing this book. Your comments were the defining things that made me keep striving even when I was sorely tempted to give up. I am especially grateful to each of you.

Sincere thanks to The Sunday Times for their permission to use photographs and articles.

Grateful thanks to Rodney Phillips - the General Manager of His Majesty's Theatre Perth - and his staff for their generosity.